The

Real Deal

The Journey of an
International Student
in the U.K.

Olanike Adebayo

ISBN: 1-4392-3149-4
ISBN-13: 9781439231494

Visit www.booksurge.com to order additional copies.

All accounts narrated in this book are entirely true experiences of the author although some names have been changed for the privacy of those involved.

Dedicated to my dear friend, a sister from another mother who bid this world goodbye without any notice. Bukola Ogun, you are always in my thoughts. Your love and words remain here with me still!

CHAPTERS AND TITLES

THE REAL DEAL:

THE JOURNEY AND TALES OF AN

INTERNATIONAL STUDENT IN THE UK

CHAPTER I
JUST LANDING

On a breezy, chilly autumn evening in late September I landed at Heathrow airport with my mum to resume attending university.

"Whao!" I muttered. "Is this the much-awaited London and the United Kingdom? Well, I am here now." I was ready to settle down into real university life.

On arrival, I had in one hand my hand luggage and in the other my portable black handbag. We were immediately directed into the security and immigration office for a checking-in and some serious questioning. On entering the office, the lady at the counter asked for my passport, which I handed over to her. She had this stern and serious look in her eyes that spoke volumes.

With a deep and serious gaze, she turned over the pages, then lifted up her face, her eyelid staring right into my eyeballs. She then turned back to the passport pages and looked again at my photograph there, then looked back at me as if she was seeing a face different from the one in the document. After a few tense minutes, she documented certain things into the computer in front of her and asked if I was the one in the picture. Asking the obvious, wasn't she?

"Yes," I replied. Did she really expect me to answer in the negative?

She interrogated me further by asking for my date of birth, purpose for being in the UK, and what the duration of my course was. I answered each question appropriately and wondered why the questioning session was on, much more since my mum wasn't subjected to the same process.

Maybe it was because I was entering the UK for the first time, or I looked too young, or whatever her reason was. As she handed my passport back to me after about fifteen minutes, I heaved a deep sigh of relief. Thank God I could now move on. My mum was waiting patiently for me so that we could retrieve our luggage from the check-out and get a cab home.

As we left the immigration post, dragging our suitcases with the last ounces of energy in us, I enquired from my mum how we would get to her apartment, and she replied that we would get a taxi once we reached the appropriate arrival terminal. To my surprise, there were lines of individuals holding name-bearing placards at the airport. These were actually the cab drivers or cab companies' representatives.

The idea is that people arriving or their relatives who reside in the UK would have booked the cab in advance, and since thousands of individuals arrive at these terminals daily, the only way to pick up the right passenger without causing any chaos was to inscribe his or her name on a placard and wait patiently for that person's arrival. Clearly, I was fast coming to grips with the fact that I was in a completely different country and a vastly different culture.

Where I am from, especially in Lagos, Nigeria, at the airport the *danfo* drivers call out their destinations, taxi drivers with their high-pitched voices screaming people's name down their throats. In Nigeria, *danfo* is a word for passenger buses and vans. They just park at the airport and beckon people to jump in, even if they hadn't booked their services. Whether they are genuine or unlicensed cab drivers is left for the passengers to figure out. In our wonderful African way, passengers are persuaded to use the cab services, and accordingly are expected to haggle over the prices. Bargaining seems to be an engrained part of African culture.

Right then, though, I had left Lagos and was in London, UK where even the cab drivers wore identification badges and registration numbers. Cab drivers or cabbies as they are known? This was really interesting. With cabbies having a regulatory body and checks, what else was I to expect? Hmm, incredible! If I thought I had seen a high level of organisation then, I was in for even greater surprises.

Anyway, lest I bore you with my taxi-and-cabbies palaver. I'll get on with my tale. We got our cab, which was waiting for us. It was a grey, seven-seat vehicle and the cabdriver was a fellow Nigerian. Our destination was South East London, and by that time it was late in the evening and getting a bit dark. The journey of almost an hour was relaxing, and I enjoyed the driver's jokes and multiple enquiries about our trip, although I honestly just wasn't in the mood for chatter myself and left him to it.

As we alighted from the cab, I watched my mum take out some notes, amounting to fifty pounds. I watched as she handed them over to the driver, who responded, "Aunty, I should charge you more, you know. The journey is pretty a long one.'.

We got into the house, and as we put down our bags I raised a big alarm. "Mum, you don't mean to say that you paid all that for a single trip, do you? Were there other expenses included?"

In response, she said that it was only a fair price for the journey from Heathrow Airport home.

I felt I had to exclaim even further, "Fifty pounds? The equivalent of ten thousand Nigerian naira? A whole ten thousand naira for a forty, forty-five minute trip?" Then I went on to say that it was nothing but a rip-off.

My mum was quick to dismiss my submission and explained that it was the cost of living in the UK. To be candid, I couldn't get my mind off the price, with my mind actively engaging itself in calculating the foreign exchange. I thought of a number of things that I could get done with ten thousand Nigerian naira. That was real serious business.

Being an average Nigerian, my aunt who shared the house with my mum had prepared a dish of rice and stew. I tasted the meat and it was really delicious. It tasted like bush meat, as we call it back in Nigeria, only to be told that it was smoked turkey. I had eaten frozen cooked turkey many times, but not this delicious smoked version of it. In case you are wondering what bush meat is, I'll give you an overview of this exquisite special delicacy that is eaten in Nigeria on particularly special occasions. By the way, I hope no animal-rights activist gets wind of this treasured information lest trouble erupts right away.

Bush meat is meat from such wild animals as antelopes, grasscutter, or deer, which are hunted in a game reserve or forest and sold for an absolute fortune. The size of the bushmeat is a sign of the hunter's expertise and experience. Trust me — it tastes yummy, or it did until I started being bombarded with these animal-rights campaigns cum wildlife reserves preservation speeches. Before that happened, as far as I was concerned it was just fine to eat bushmeat and then desire more.

In case you'd really care to know what it is like, I'd advise you to visit certain eateries in my native country. As long as you don't go there with an arrest warrant or caution and you don't campaign for the rights of the poor, helpless animals, there won't be a problem. Until I came into the UK, I never knew that even hamsters had legislative rights. Dogs, cats, rabbits, donkeys, and on a lighter note, cockroaches and maybe grasshoppers have rights which no human dares tamper with.

OUT AND ABOUT

During the first few days of settling down and arranging my stuff, it began to dawn on me that I was in a different world entirely. My mum and I had gone out to visit some friends and to do some shopping. By the way, the instant conversions and calculations of the exchange rate were still deeply ingrained in me at that stage. I kept converting the prices to naira before embarking on any purchase.

We went to some shopping malls a few days after my arrival and I was in awe of what they looked like. Even though I had been to shopping arcades and malls in Nigeria, they were nothing like the ones I visited in London. There were no hawkers pressing their goods into our hands, no by-side displays, no rhythmical, comical, loud advertisements from a microphone, no fierce competition between the sellers to attract customers, and not even the pep-talks meant to persuade us to go into a shop. To crown it all, there was no haggling and bargaining over prices.

The prices were fixed and all we had to do was to pay. The whole shopping experience was so un-African. The main excitement of shopping back home was in the practice of bargaining and the sweet-tongued persuasions from the sellers.

Everything was so well arranged, and the items for sale were freely displayed in the stores without anybody necessarily looking. Trust me, if it were in some of the places I knew, shoplifters could easily walk in and make away with those wares on display. I kept wondering if the shop owners were being plain stupid, not security conscious, or careless. These questions and many more raced through my mind as we moved from store to store.

What I didn't realise at the time was that most of the stores had closed-circuit television (CCTV) cameras installed to catch out thieves and shoplifters, and all the items were electronically tagged so that any attempt to make away with anything without paying would sound an alarm to the security crew on duty.

The main thing that bothered me at the time was the fixed prices for everything. That there was no way of beating down the prices seemed to pose a serious concern to me. Imagine my thoughts at the time! Why was I expecting price bargains when I was not in an auction house where prices are negotiated?

To complicate matters for the foreigner in me, even fish, poultry, meat, and groceries sold in open markets had fixed prices. The items would be weighed on a scale and the price would be determined. I must admit that I have successfully bargained for some items in the open markets and have received some discounts.

I couldn't understand how I would survive in this new world, having lived all my life in a system where the economics of the marketplace is based on a person's bargaining power. Being able to beat prices down could even ensure that I had favourites among the sellers.

In an average Nigerian market, if an item is said to be a thousand naira, a person could end up beating down the price to as little as two hundred or three hundred naira. The real worth of the item is hardly the price placed on it at first. People who are not good at bargaining can end up paying as much as twice or triple the real worth.

Realising that I was in a different system, I knew that I had to adapt fast and leave the familiar marketplace I was used to. If you're in Rome, you have to behave like a Roman. Here was I in the UK, and I had to act like a British resident.

In the shopping mall I got the materials I needed for survival in the terrible cold: 100-denier-thick tights (the denier number signifies the thickness), a pair of trainers, a pair of gloves, a scarf with a matching hat, and pairs of socks. After shopping, my mum and I retreated into a café for some hot drinks. The price for two cups of hot drinks and two slices of cake was around five pounds. I immediately converted how much that would be in naira and insisted that I didn't want any. As far as I was concerned, it was too expensive. That would have been about a thousand Nigerian naira. I insisted to my mum that I would rather have the money and have a cup of hot drink when we got home. She tried explaining to me that that was the cost of living in the UK and that I wasn't doing myself any justice by denying myself what I needed.

Before reeling out in laughter, you need to understand how much that meant to me at the time as an undergraduate from a Nigerian university. If the international students' fees were that expensive, it was still understandable. At least the fees were for a tangible and worthy cause, but what about a cup of tea, which I thought would have been cheap? I eventually succumbed to the persuasion instead of suffering in the chilly cold and took the two-pounds-and-fifty-pence café treat.

After having the hot drink, which I considered to be a treat, we went out to see a friend of my mum's. I was wearing one of my mum's winter jackets, which the woman frowned at immediately we entered her office. She asked why I was wearing an old-fashioned jacket which wasn't meant for my age group. She asked her daughter to take me to the nearby mall to buy a trendy and fashionable jacket for me.

I was as clueless as my mum that I was wearing the wrong kind of jacket. Looking back now, I wonder how on earth I wore that granny-style jacket confidently around the sophisticated city of London until my mum's friend intervened.

We spent the next few days shopping and visiting friends and relatives in London. Since I had a firm offer from the University of Bradford, I started preparing for the journey. Neither my mum nor I knew how far Bradford was from London. All we knew was that it was a city in the north of England far from London, which is situated in the southern part of the country.

Fortunately, we contacted one of my cousins, who lived in nearby Leeds. When I informed him of my move to Bradford University he became enthusiastic about my university of choice, which is known for the excellent practical skills and knowledge base it imparts to its students. My cousin confirmed that the motto of the university, Making Knowledge Work, was true.

I don't know what I was thinking, but I had made no concrete arrangement for university accommodation at that stage. I believed that I would get a room in one of the halls of residence, since the university promised to reserve a room on campus for all new intakes. My cousin, Ola, asked me to get down to Bradford the next day because the university had opened for students' registration and orientation.

FAREWELL LONDON

The next day, which was a Wednesday, my mum took me to Victoria Coach Station. I bought a return ticket to Leeds and boarded the coach later in the afternoon. Since Bradford is only a twenty-minute commute to Leeds, Ola assured me that I could commute easily from Leeds for university registration and the first weeks of lectures. The journey to Leeds seemed like eternity for the five or so hours that it took. My first thought was that the coach had a mechanical fault due to the extremely slow speed at which it moved. I was sure that it was travelling at a speed of no more than 80 km/hr. Being used to the Nigerian transport system, in which coaches go around 100 to 120 km/hr, this slow-coach system was weird to me. Is it any wonder that there are so few road-accident casualties in the UK?

As I kept wondering why the coach was so slow, I couldn't but wonder why the speed seemed to be all right to everyone else on board. To me, it seemed to be an absolute waste of time. The journey could simply have been made shorter in duration. Strangely, the driver continually made different announcements via the tannoy system. The first announcement was that the coach would stop for a short break, the next when a change of driver was due, followed by where the onboard toilet was located.

It was even more surprising that a five to five-and-a-half-hour journey wasn't made by a single driver, but by two different ones. I knew of ten-hour journeys back in Nigeria that are made by a single driver, with only a few breaks in between. At that time I didn't understand the rationale behind the breaks and the driver switch. It felt like everything in this new country was different to what I knew life to be.

At last we arrived at Leeds City Bus Station. It was late in the evening. Even though it was only about 7.00 pm, the darkness in the sky was as thick as a man's fist. As I alighted from the coach I experienced the intensity of the cold weather. I later got to understand that the farther north a person travels in the UK, the colder it becomes, so a city like Leeds is naturally colder than London. Bradford, being further north still from Leeds, is yet colder. Knowing about weather changes taught me to check the weather forecast, either on the internet or on the news, before embarking on any journey outside my location.

Ola knew beforehand when my coach would arrive in Leeds and he was right there waiting. We hugged each other and exchanged pleasantries while he led me to his car. He grabbed my medium-sized green suitcase and placed it in his car's boot. It was great seeing him after a number of years apart. As we got into conversations, my inquisitive mind got me asking him a million and one questions about my observations in the UK.

My first set of questions was about the weather, the transport system, the slow-running coach that seemed to be crawling more than moving, university life, and the queuing up system, which I later got to understand is one of the main points of British etiquette. It surprised me that the books I had read about the UK prior to my arrival had not contained a lot of the things I was experiencing. The nitty-gritty of British life wasn't something I knew about at all.

CHAPTER 2
JOURNEY JUST COME (JJC)

The day following my arrival in Leeds, Ola drove me round to
see Leeds's boisterous city centre and the universities there. Seeing the
city in broad daylight was different to the scenery I saw on my arrival.
Even though the Leeds city centre was relatively busy, it wasn't as alive
and busy as London. Maybe manic would be the appropriate word to
describe London in comparison with Leeds.

After driving around Leeds for a bit we went off to Bradford.
We found our way easily to the university from the motorway and
headed for the international office. If I thought that Leeds was calm,
Bradford appeared to be even calmer. Once at the student registration
department, I introduced myself to the officer in charge as a new
student and he handed me a registration pack. After all my documents
had been verified, I was immediately issued a student identity badge.
It was different to the system I came from, where the identity badge
was only issued weeks after registering at university. Ola and I went
to the Department of Biomedical Science, where I completed the
departmental registration and received a brief orientation, since I had
missed the orientation week.

I didn't know what the orientation week entailed, and so hadn't
considered it important enough to attend. Now I totally agree with the
university authorities that the orientation week is an integral programme

that all students, most importantly the international students, need in order to settle into the system.

Unknown to me, lectures had fully commenced during the week that I arrived in the UK. I was told to attend classes immediately after I finished with the necessary registration processes in order to catch up with the lectures. There I was, a student from a Nigerian university where the date of resumption only refers to the day we arrive on campus for catching up and socialising with our mates, certainly not for starting lectures that same week. It could take a few weeks before we commenced classes seriously. I couldn't understand what the rush was all about at this university.

As a proper Journey Just Come (JJC), I was all wrapped up in like four layers of clothing, thick gloves, a scarf, and a hat. That was the coldest weather I had experienced until that time. I can imagine I looked somewhat strange to some of the people who came across me, like an Eskimo or someone from the North Pole, but as long as I was warm and okay, who cares what the public's opinions were?

Surprisingly, I saw many female students in long flowing robes, scarves, and headveils moving around on campus. My curious self was quick to ask Ola what they were doing around the university campus. It looked like I was in northern Nigeria, where Sharia law is practised, or in the Arab world. Ola explained to me that they were all university students like me. More than fifty percent of the students on campus were of either Pakistani or Indian ancestry. Bradford's multicultural nature is reflected in the ethnic diversity of the students, too. Bradford, being home to one of the highest Asian populations in the UK, is often referred to as the country's curry capital. I bet you couldn't get better curry elsewhere in the UK.

On the same day that I registered at the students' registration department, I was issued a letter of introduction which I presented at the NatWest Bank on campus in order to open an account in my name. the bank's customer-service assistant was quick to attend to me as soon as I arrived, taking my personal details and verifying my identity by taking a photocopy of my passport.

I realised that as an immigrant I would always need my passport as proof of my identity. It's only a matter of safety for all international students to have their passport with them for the first few weeks after arriving in the country. Most public offices demand to see our passports before attending to us.

It was great opening a bank account in my first week at university. I believed it was fine until I realised later that the type of account to which I had access was without many of the privileges given to home students, such as a chequebook and other offers. As I found out from other international students, though, not all banks had these bottleneck regulations. Only a few operated in this manner.

It is therefore worthwhile to ask questions about the benefits and privileges that come with opening an account with a bank before doing so. In my opinion, it was clearly unfair to all the international students concerned, as we bring a huge amount of resources into the UK banking system, as much as the home students, actually, if not more.

The transfers of our fees and monthly stipends, totalling thousands of pounds, operate from these accounts. It is only proper for the banks concerned to accord us suitable respect, rather than treating us as second-class customers.

If an international student spends as many as three or four years in the country, I would have thought that good interest rates and offers should be made available to that individual. In contrast, my bank account as a student was being taxed more highly than the interest it generated. If I wasn't gaining from an account, I could at least be left with the funds I placed inside, but that's not the taxation system in this country.

After a long day of crash lectures, student registry, and bank registration, we headed back to Leeds, which would be my base for a few more weeks.

GREEN AND NAÏVE

My highly green and naïve self was fast adjusting to the UK weather and lifestyle and with university life. My humorous cousin and his wife Kerry didn't make matters better with their mythically cooked-up tales, which I lapped up like a hungry dog. Much of the information they gave me was true, but not without them taking the mickey out of me at first. As I had missed university orientation, they gave me a bespoke orientation that helped me in getting my feet on the ground.

The first rule in getting by was "Look very well to your ways in this country," meaning that I should check things properly before believing or giving in to them, as many offers seem gold-plated but are fake. If it sounds too good to be true, in most cases it is. Furthermore, most things that are offered for free aren't usually free, but are likely to be covers for hidden agendas.

True to their words, I had my first taste of the butty in my first few weeks of classes. I walked into the student union building to familiarise myself with the environment and found some free postcards. We were told to pick up as many as we wanted. Since they were freebies, I picked up a few, which I intended to use for writing to my mum and a few friends. Good enough, I showed them to my cousin, who became hysterical upon seeing the inscription and words on them.

Needless to say, the colloquial words on the postcards, which I didn't understand, were vulgar and outright inappropriate for using to write to my mum, or to any decent friend for that matter. One had an inscription with words connoting a "Moonie". I didn't know what a Moonie was and obviously hadn't looked closely at the postcard's boldly inscribed picture, which depicted a Moonie as a drunken man who takes off his clothes and dances showing his bottom to the amusement of onlookers.

By this time, lesson number one was getting instilled into me firmly. Ola and Kerry firmly re-emphasised the rule of looking to my ways well and not taking just anything on board.

Paramount lesson number two was that "Big Brother is there watching," *Big Brother* being a term to describe the CCTV cameras located in most public places in the UK. From lecture theatres to the corridors, to the foyer and even in toilets, a CCTV is there covering all that goes on. From what I know, the cameras aren't installed exactly inside toilet cubicles, but only in the waiting areas. If big brother were to be in toilet cubicles it would be a ridiculously interesting matter.

Did I just say *toilet*? A slip of the tongue? No, sorry, the slip of the keyboard. Toilets are referred to as loos, bathrooms or the ladies'. Those synonyms for toilet are considered to be the prudish and discrete words for referring to it, but, let's face it, what is wrong with the word 'toilet'? I'd leave that idea for anyone interested to decipher.

This orientation session was going on fine until we got to the next lesson, which was to reduce the volume from the house to the barest minimum. If the neighbours felt uncomfortable with the television volume, loud voice pitches, or music, they might get the police and the local council involved. I laughed as hard as I could because I thought they were exaggerating the claim.

That was one of the strangest things I had heard in a long time. That neighbours would not address their fellows in a friendly manner about the displeasure but get the authorities involved was beyond belief. I grew up in a society where neighbours form a close-knit community, such that one would pop into the other's house without notice and vice-versa. Again, I was coming to terms with not being in Africa.

Here, neighbours are only considered to be the person living next door. There is no more to the relationship than residing in the same vicinity. I was always cautioned to lower my voice because of the neighbours. With little or no relating with neighbours, I came to understand why people often complain of loneliness and isolation. If the phrase, "Love your neighbour as yourself," is to be taken literally, it should be in the UK.

The orientation lessons were getting better. I received pieces of information no book would have provided. Another such lesson was to ask questions directly from authority if I was ever in doubt. Any attempt not to do this could result in being misinformed. Even if I didn't understand what a lecturer said, I should feel free to walk up to him or her and ask for clarity, and if the need be ask for extra tuition on the subject area. That felt a bit daunting, especially since I wasn't used to dealing freely with lecturers. Where I was from only a few lecturers are easily approachable. The majority of them are treated as demigods or goddesses.

I must admit that the enthusiasm with which lecturers in the UK relate to their students is sometimes overwhelming. We don't need to be privileged to talk to them, ask questions about their on-going research, or even about their personal lives. Believe me, I utilised that privilege to the maximum. If anything else didn't give me the audacity, the exorbitant fees I paid were enough reason to get all I could out of the system.

As long as a student does not abuse the privilege, having easy access to lecturers is one of the best things to happen to us since sliced bread. Having started classes late, plus being a second-year entrant, I had a backlog of work to catch up on. Getting extra help from the lecturers was a real plus at that point.

My wonderful cousin and his wife never gave up on their pranks and fairy tales. I really had a swell time for the duration I stayed at their house. I knew that part of British culture was keeping pets inside the house, at times in the bedroom, but I had never imagined myself ever living with one. Not being such a pet enthusiast, I politely asked if Ola and Kerry kept a cat, dog, or any pet for that matter. The shocking answer I got was that they actually did, but it was an uncommon pet, a pet python. With serious trepidation and a sense of concern, I started to devise a way to escape from the people that housed a pet snake.

Before I learnt of the pet snake, the plan was to commute to Bradford from Leeds for a few weeks until I found a nice accommodation near campus. It was bad enough to live with a pet, but how could I bear the thought of living with a snake? That thought by itself disturbed me.

Ola and Kerry knew the effect their snake tale would have on me, so they painted the image more graphically. They said that the snake was allowed into the house sometimes, especially if they had a visitor, and that it would often stick its neck out to the guest as a sign of friendliness. Not knowing that they were playing a fast one on me, I decided to notify my mum that I was moving back to London. She had always wanted me to attend a London university, anyway, and there couldn't have been a better opportunity to grab that option.

After a while, they told me the truth and were surprised that I could fall for such a dumb joke. How wouldn't I? They'd appeared to be dead serious, and their story was completely coherent. At the end of the day, this is the UK, where anything is potentially possible.

KOSHER FOODS

At the same time that Ola and Kerry were getting me oriented, I learnt about some other cultures that I had known little or nothing about. Along their street in Leeds was a corner off-license shop, which I patronised regularly. During my first few weeks in the UK, I got hooked on chocolates and would often dash into the shop for some bars.

On one occasion I needed to get a few grocery items but didn't want to bother going as far as the supermarket. I thought that I could grab a few items from the corner shop, although the prices were likely to be a bit more expensive than at the major supermarket. To my surprise, some of the prices were as much as twice the supermarkets' prices. I decided to ask the friendly shopkeeper why the prices were that high, and his response was that most of the dairy and meat products were kosher.

I didn't know what kosher meant at the time, or what the name implied for the prices. On further asking what that meant, he explained that kosher is the name given to foods eaten by the Jews. The foods are said to be ceremonially clean according to certain Jewish rites, which make them more expensive than other products.

Up until that time, I didn't realise that the area where I lived in Leeds had a large Jewish community, and that meant that most of the corner shops in the area sold kosher food products. That was another learning experience for me, to know that certain ethnic groups had different purifications for their food products. I never knew that Jews were that strict with their everyday ways of life, extending as far as the food they eat.

෬〇

CHAPTER 3
MULTICULTURAL UNITED KINGDOM, HERE I COME!

If only I'd had more detailed information about the cultural settings, mindsets, and multicultural nature of the UK, maybe I wouldn't have been as shocked as I was upon my arrival into the country. Most of my former beliefs were being questioned, confronting me right in the face. I had gathered, probably by assumption as well, from my history and geography classes back in school that the UK is mainly inhabited by native Caucasians, only to meet people from many different racial and ethnic origins once there.

My ordeal with this started when I left the plane at Heathrow airport, where I saw a number of Chinese people, blacks, and Arabs. There were women wearing long covering robes and veils covering their faces. I thought that they might be just visitors, only to discover that what I saw was the real representation of the ethnic groups residing in the country.

That was only the tip of the iceberg. Then I arrived in the main city of London. My goodness!! What a mix of black African, black Caribbean, Chinese, Latinos, Indians, Pakistanis, Bangladeshis, and whites from every part of Europe and the world. In my mind, I was still asking if this really was the UK I had read so much about.

As time went by, I discovered that London, said to be the most multicultural and cosmopolitan city in the world, with different people from a vast number of countries, is a defining city as far as multiculturalism is concerned.

If London gave me such a shock, I was in for ruder shocks when I visited Manchester, Leeds, and Bradford, my university city. Both Manchester and Leeds have notably high numbers of Pakistani and Afro-Caribbean people who have settled in the UK for up to three or four generations. These groups know nowhere else other than the UK as home.

To be honest, as I saw and observed them they couldn't have been less British. Other than such Asian and African cultural factors as food, dressing, and family life having been inculcated into their lives here in the UK, they were British through and through.

Bradford, on the other hand, was a totally different kettle of fish. On turning up at the university for my student registration, I observed that a very large percentage of the student population, maybe up to forty percent, were of Pakistani or Indian origin, and students of such ethnic minorities as Chinese, other Asians, blacks, Mediterraneans, and others actually made up over fifty percent of those at the university. The diverse mix of students at Bradford University makes it stand out from most other universities in the UK. I doubt if any other university in the UK could actually beat that record.

Ladies in long, covered-up robes with veils were a common sight, as were guys dressed like they do in the Middle East. If I hadn't been convinced that I had boarded a flight to the UK,

I would have been tempted to believe that I was in another country altogether.

Also, many of the inhabitants of Bradford are from the Caribbean. The families of many of them had settled there in the days of the Bradford textile industry boom in the nineteenth and early twentieth centuries, which gave it the nickname of the British Textile Capital then. The boom brought a mass influx of workers, mainly from India, Pakistan, and the Caribbean islands of Jamaica, Trinidad, and Dominica. Unfortunately, an economic crisis arising from increased competition from India, Southeast Asia, and the Far East led to the downfall of Bradford's great and prosperous textile industry. By that time, however, Bradford had succeeded in gathering the multiethnic character which it still maintains.

If there was anything I came to value and appreciate highly in Bradford, it was this multi-cultural view of life that it offers. Ranging from British food to African, from Caribbean to Indian curries and fashion houses, Bradford offers these competitively in different arrays and display. No wonder it is known as the curry capital of the United Kingdom. I sure can testify to that.

Before I go on about foods and curries, I'll get back to the multi- cultural UK and the culture shock which most international students, myself included, experienced without end.

The number of Chinese students in UK universities was utterly unbelievable. I guess for a country like China, with a population of over one billion people, a few hundred Chinese students on a university campus would definitely be an insignificant number.

Whatever the case was, I was enjoying the multicultural institution to which I belonged.

FASHION AND DRESS SENSE

My presumption of fashion in the UK was to meet ladies in high-heeled shoes, pencil skirts, properly buttoned blouses, and well-set hair, as I had seen in various British movies. The men? Nice pin-stripe suits, fitted shirts with matching ties, cufflinks, and formal shoes – or better still, formal shirts tucked into the pair of trousers. Was I in for disappointments!

Other than some lawyers, bankers, managers, and medical doctors, most professionals just dressed casually, though smart enough for work, and even in some cases a bit more informally than the dress sense in Nigeria.

In Nigeria, people are expected to be dressed formally for work in skirt or trouser suits, ties, and formal shoes. I realised that the way people dress in the UK is rather laid back and not exactly formal. In my home country, students have to make an effort in dressing for lectures – casual but smart. I realised that the usual clothing here is totally different, with jeans, hooded tops, jumpers, t-shirts, cardigans, trainers, and boots the order of the day.

University college students are unlikely to be seen in formal shirts or blouses. Jeans and hoodies could be described as the students' official wear or uniforms. The incredible thing to me is how tattered and rough the jeans could be, not to mention the rugged and dirty states of some of the trainers.

Funny enough, most of the Asian students hardly wore Western clothes. They came to classes in their traditional Indian or Pakistani clothing. The expensive accessories they came with made me wonder how students could afford that much. A few odd times they would wear jeans and knitted wear, but they tended to stick strongly to their traditional costumes. Talk of having a strong sense of ethnic identity!

In case you're wondering, as I did, what 'jumpers' are, they are certainly not mid-rib tops but knitted, mostly turtleneck ones. For the winter, which lasts from around December till early March, jumpers are the most practical outfits for making it through the harsh cold and snow. Cardigans and other thick clothes are needed mostly for the autumn season, which lasts from the end of September to December – all things being equal, with the British weather being consistently inconsistent.

Having arrived from a tropical country at a northern university at the end of September, I thought that was the coldest time of the year. You should have seen me with my thinsulate gloves and hat (the thickest material available), heavy fur jacket, and three to four layers of clothes.

First would be thermal underwear, covered with a jumper, a cardigan on top, and finally my winter jacket. Not once did I forget to wear my woollen scarf tightly around my neck for warmth. Being used to my light t-shirts and clothing which I could no longer wear, it felt like I was being subjected to a punishment with these layered outfits.

Living in a different dress culture where boots and tights are worn daily to keep the cold off was the start of getting to grips with my new way of life.

As much as I complained about the weather and wrapping up to ward off the cold, I was terrified to see how some students would go out late in the night in skimpy outfits. Some of the dresses would show their bare backs and would cover no more than the upper parts of their thighs. I never ceased to wonder how they coped with that chilling cold, especially with Bradford being colder than most of the cities surrounding it, as its rocky and hilly nature means that it gets colder than nearby Leeds or Huddersfield. The higher it gets, the colder it becomes.

Prior to living in the UK, I was used to defining people's identity and nationality by their appearance. Once I moved over here, that proved to be shallow and sometimes untrue. I met students who appeared in form and appearance as Indians, but enquiries on where they were from brought the funny answer of "Here," meaning the UK. I met some other people who were of Caribbean or Chinese descent. Up until then, I had never known that there were people classified as Black British, Pakistani British, or Chinese British.

The only classifications of the typical appearances are referred to as their ancestry, meaning where their parents or grandparents or more distant ancestors came from. In reality, being British-born and bred gives them a Western identity and mindset. Although some still hold on religiously to the attitudes and identities of their country of descent, being born and brought up in the UK makes them completely British.

Classifying a person's identity based on her or his appearance is actually considered to be rude, so to be on the safer side it's always better to ask the question, if in doubt, "Where are you from?" A sense of identity with a place or country is something people treasure highly. Any attempt to rob an individual of that identity would not be taken with levity. I learnt that the hard way, though.

I met a Muslim lady at university who appeared to be of Pakistani or Middle Eastern origin. She even had an Asian-sounding name. As I introduced myself as being a fellow student from Nigeria, I expected her to say that she was from India or Pakistan or somewhere in the Middle East, but to my utmost dismay she told me that she was from Manchester.

Without the understanding I now have of identity and origin, I probed her further as to why she claimed to be a Mancunian, which is what people born and bred in Manchester are called. Her response, with a bit of irritation, was, "Because that's where I'm from, and where do you expect me to be from, anyway?"

I was forced to explain immediately my Nigerian presumptions about the UK. My impression at the time was that this country was mainly made up of Caucasians, and those who were of different racial origins did not identify themselves as being British. Now all those ideas were evaporating as light was shed.

In reality, how else could we define someone who knows no other place as home, since two or three generations of their family have been permanently resident in a country? It is only fair for them to be identified as bonafide British people as long as they are contributing to the smooth running of their communities and society at large. Although we'd hear of some white Britishers who act in a radically prejudiced manner, passing ugly and derogatory comments about ethnic-minority Brits and using statements like, "Go back to your country" or "We don't want you here" to communicate their bigotry.

In the same way that people can't refer to white South Africans as being less African, it is unreasonable and incorrect to ascertain a person's identity or citizenship by shallow standards. Do people tell a white South African or even an English-speaking one to return to his country of origin, when actually South Africa has been home for many generations?

Indeed, a person's identity and culture have an element of parental origin, but much more; the environment in which we are brought up has a larger impact. Many of my ethnic-minority British friends are thoroughly British in their thinking and attitudes, though they would hardly agree totally with that notion. Still, their attitudes to money, to the legal system and being able to exercise their rights, and their accents are completely Westernised, yet in spite of their Britishness, their religious influences can actually make a great deal of difference in their ways of life.

A majority of the Asians that I came in contact with were Muslims, Hindus, or Sikhs of Pakistani or Indian ancestry and have a strong sense of family cohesion and values. They live together in large houses with extended members of the family, run jointly-owned family businesses, and raise their children with the same values. Of course, there are always exceptions to the rule, but they generally regard and prize family relationships highly.

Even though they may strictly adhere to an Islamic way of life, the general British laws still override Sharia. As I interacted with many British Muslims, I discovered some intriguing yet interesting cultures. One of the first things that shocked me was that they only eat Halal food.

Halal food, mainly meat and poultry, has been prepared to strict Islamic guidelines, which means that prayers are said over the animals and they are slaughtered by bleeding rather than by chemical or electrical means. I realised that these friends of mine would not eat any burgers, chicken, or food in many fast food joints like McDonalds, Burger King, or KFC.

At first I thought that they weren't interested in eating meat, as they only requested vegetarian dishes at the university refectory. I asked my classmate Salima why she had once again opted for the vegetarian menu and she explained to me that she wasn't a vegetarian, but only ate Halal food. Who could have known that with a modern, Westernised way of life, British-born Muslims still adhere strictly to their religion and all the rites involved?

They still wear veils, maintain strict male-female relations, eat only Halal food, and observe the prayer times. I thought that most of those Islamic tenets were only practised religiously in the Middle East and the Arab world. Anyway, I think it's interesting to see the fusion of both Western and Islamic cultures being inculcated and evident in these people. What is more surprising is that these folks have lived all their lives in the UK, yet have such strong sense of commitment to their faith and their ethnic cultures.

Another extremely shocking discovery for me was that consanguine, arranged, and forced marriages existed amongst a number of Asian British people. Many of these young Asian girls in my year at the university were already married, some as young as eighteen. More shocking was that most of these marriages were arranged by their parents and families, and if that wasn't strange enough to me, their spouses were mostly their first cousins.

My close colleague Rabeana mentioned how she had spoken over the phone to her first cousin on a number of occasions after she was made aware of the arrangement between the parents on both sides. She further told me that she saw his pictures and communicated via instant messaging and telephone, and that they got married when she travelled to Pakistan on holiday.

I rebuffed her for cracking such an expensive joke on me and asked her to tell me her true love story. She maintained that what she had told me was the truth, the whole truth, and nothing but the truth. If I was really in doubt, she would have some other ladies in the class who had similar love and marriage stories narrate theirs to me.

I was still aghast with surprise when she beckoned to them, and two other ladies confirmed that what she said was true and that it was similar to their own experiences.

"No," I exclaimed. "Not in the twenty-first century, and certainly not in a first-world country like the UK. An arranged marriage? No real contacts? Parental involvement? To a first cousin?"

These things were just outright unbelievable. "Not even in the part of Africa where I'm from would you find such practices," I continued. "Oh my! I'm indeed in a different sphere and world."

At that stage I was more than inquisitive about why such practices, which I termed old-fashioned, outdated, and barbaric, were being enforced on them. To my utter dismay, they were just fine with it and didn't think about the set-up as I did. Here I come, England! This was a major educational discovery for me, as I was elaborately educated and lectured on the ins and outs of the practices.

They also explained why they believed in such practices in spite of their Western education, environment, and upbringing. They see arranged marriages as a means of furthering family unity, believing that only close family members such as cousins could have their best interests at heart. They believe that if cousins can be married to each other, the family's love, assets, and bonds would be preserved.

Since charity is said to begin at home, the young ones in the family are taught these values from an early age, so that as they enter into adolescence and adulthood they have been instilled as the normal way of life. Since being romantically inclined towards my cousin is beyond me, I found it difficult to accept the practice as normal, or as other than incest.

Even though some organisations campaign against the encouragement of such consanguine marriages, many young and enlightened British Asians still believe that the tradition should be upheld and propagated. On the other hand, some who have seen their detrimental health consequences preach against it. The grounds for opposition are usually based on the widespread presence of genetic diseases, which are continuously inherited by the children bred in such relationships.

As a scientist, I could understand and identify clearly with the second school of thought. The probability of defective genes being passed down to future generations is higher in consanguine marriages than in those who marry out of their local gene pool.

Those who believe in consanguine marriages are of the opinion that marrying into the same extended family unit promotes the unity and love within it, believing that this tradition further strengthens the family ties which are paramount to them. More than anything, something that stands out and which I have come to respect personally in Indian and Pakistani people is their respect for the family unit. They exemplify the importance of family members to one another's wellbeing.

The importance of the family unit is firmly instilled in family members and passed down the generations. They understand a functional family to be the basic unit and bedrock of society. It is reasonable to accept that this notion is pivotal to the Asian communities' successes and entrepreneurial achievements. Every coin has two sides, though, and the negative outcomes of tightly-controlled family units have been known to be disastrous.

It was not surprising to hear of young women who are forced into marriages arranged by their parents or other male family members. At first, it sounded absolutely ridiculous for me to hear about these events. A typical example of this was a colleague of mine, Aisha, who was visibly depressed. As we got into discussions, she mentioned how her older brother and cousins were mounting pressure on her to marry this cousin of theirs whom she had met on only two occasions. She had declined to give her consent to this demand. Disobedience to the family amounted to gross dishonour as far as the other members of the family were concerned. Since she had put the family to shame, the price to pay for her decision was excommunication.

What a dilemma to force upon a young lady whose main support mechanism throughout her life had been her family! In a bid to be accepted and treated as a bonafide member of the family, she gave in to marrying a man who could be described as a familiar stranger. This is just a typical example of how strong family influence conflicts with the personal choices and desires of some.

If Aisha's story isn't compelling enough, I can assure you that this next one should move your heart with compassion. A young lady I met on my part-time job, Nisha, was a divorcee when I met her. She was working really hard to keeps herself together at that stage of her life and was absolutely not going to give marriage a place in her heart because of the many hurts she had experienced in the past.

Born and bred in Pakistan, her male cousin had asked her parents for her hand in marriage without consulting her. All she knew was that in a few days time she was going to be married to her cousin, who had just arrived from the UK. As demanded, she had to play ball throughout the ceremony, bid her immediate family goodbye, and head for a supposed rosy life abroad.

Imagine having to leave behind all friendships, all emotional family ties, and her familiar environment within a week. Worse still, she had to leave her country and home for an absolute stranger, all in the name of marriage – abroad.

On arriving in the UK, she was welcomed into the new family, which seemed great, only to discover that she was basically grounded in the house, with little or no link to the outside world. The only times that she was allowed out were when her husband took her out for shopping or to the odd social event.

Having to live with a man who was an absentee husband, who left the house early in the morning and arrived late at night, coupled with some beatings from him whenever she disagreed with him, made her contact some women's helpline charity organisation, which bailed her out.

She told me she was placed in a public hostel for some months, and since she had no qualifications whatsoever she was forced to live on the government's aid. She went through an English course, since she could only communicate in her local languages, and eventually trained as a care support worker. She eventually got a job in a nursing home, where I met her as a colleague.

It was almost unbelievable to consider the nightmare she had been subjected to. Nisha's horrendous experience gave me a good example of what some ladies could be subjected to in these forced and arranged marriages. What was more mind-boggling about the whole maltreatment and ordeal was that her in in-laws were actually blood family members. In time I met different women with similar experiences, and here I was, being introduced to different cultural ethnic shocks I never could have imagined.

During my few years at university I became familiar with such stories and even more distressing ones. Another phenomenon I got to understand was the issue of honour killings. Honour killing occurs when male members of the family decide to kill their sisters or cousins for refusing the extended family's choice of marriage. Learning about them dealt another blow to my face.

These people usually consider a refusal to co-operate with the family to be a terrible shame and dishonour to the family. For such an offence of high treason against the family, the lady in question is made to pay the ultimate price: death. It is believed that the death of such ladies is more tolerable than being allowed to live for her own choices. Woe betide that lady who chooses from a group other than the family's circle. That is considered to be a no-no! Hearing of such traditions in the news wasn't just bizarre to my hearing, but also deeply disturbing.

THE UNITED KINGDOM, GREAT BRITIAN

The United Kingdom is comprised of the four countries of England, Wales, Scotland, and Northern Ireland. Great Britain, on the other hand, is comprised of only the first three, excluding Northern Ireland. London, being the capital of England as a nation, happens also to be the capital of the United Kingdom and Great Britain. Since many people tend to get confused when mentioning Britain, thinking it is mainly London, It is good to know what is really what.

London is said to be the most cosmopolitan and multicultural city in the world, and also brags about itself as one of the most expensive cities in the world to live in. It is certainly one of the most exciting cities to live in. In terms of social events, tourist attractions, and educational institutions, no city in the UK can actually beat London to it.

As I have come to understand, London is the heartbeat of the country. Everything that goes on in the UK has its hub in the city of London, be it positive or negative. Talk of the stock market, business opportunities, and the European economic capital, and London would be the first city to be mentioned. In the same vein, gun crime, stabbings, gangsters, and wildness are more rampant in the capital. London as a city has this multifacetedness to it that keeps it rolling

Canary Wharf, the equivalent of Wall Street in New York, is where the financial strength of the nation lies. It can be well put that those money matters that affect the nation and the globe are thrashed out in Canary Wharf. Such financial companies as JP Morgan, the HFC bank, the Bank of England, Have their bases in canary wharf and the city. This is where people meet the so-called big boys and girls of London, who earn extremely fat incomes and of course have the extravagant lifestyles to show for their pay packets.

TOURISM IN LONDON

The tourist places to visit in London are too numerous to enumerate. For a great day out in London, it is worthwhile to plan ahead because of the city's hustle and bustle. The London sightseeing companies offer a great sightseeing tour of the city with their open-roofed double-decker buses. The tourists just have to be fortunate that the weather stays beautiful throughout their trip. The rides are usually to famous places like Piccadilly Circus and Trafalgar Square, the famous site commemorating Lord Nelson's victory over Napoleon's navy at the Battle of Trafalgar.

The art galleries, Hyde Park Corner, Buckingham Palace, the science museum, the Tower Bridge, and London Bridge are other places to visit. A few days of tours around London are worth the while for any tourist, or any international student who doesn't want to spend all her or his precious time in the UK engrossed only in academics and university life. Part of being educated in a foreign land consists of knowing its cultural heritage and monumental sites.

For me, places like Buckingham Palace, Trafalgar Square, the National Gallery, the fashion display gallery in the National Portrait Gallery, Apsley House next to the famous and stunning Hyde Park, and the British Museum were landmarks that I had the chance to see. The best time to see the beauty and grandeur of Buckingham Palace is in the summer between July and September, when the royal family is off to their holiday home in Scotland. That's when the palace is open to the general public as a tourist attraction.

In Buckingham Palace, seeing the Royal Guards in their full regalia, the Horse Guards, their changeover ceremony when another set of guards takes over from those on duty, and all the picturesque displays that go on during the summer is a sight to behold. Believe me, the sights aren't only interesting and stimulating, but enormously impressive. They reminded me of how certain traditions have been preserved over the years and centuries.

Obviously, getting into the palace costs a reasonable price, but it is definitely worth it. Other interesting sights not to be missed are Westminster Abbey and St Paul's Cathedral. Both are monumental churches with striking historical stories and pictures.

The London Eye, London Bridge, the Tower of London, and the Museum of Science and Technology, where tourists can view the technological developments of several centuries, are other attractions.

Lest I forget, visiting Madame Tussauds, with its waxed images of the world's celebrities, is a proof of being a real tourist in London. Strike a pose with any one of them, be it the queen or the famous actors or Princess Diana, then pretend that you actually met those people in person. How else could a person easily take personalised pictures with renowned celebrities? If being an international student doesn't give a person access into the Queen's living room or Prince William's private quarters, we sure can have a splendid time with their cast wax images in Madam Tussauds.

A visit to Harrods Departmental Stores on Knightsbridge isn't just a shopping time out but a visit to a store that is a one-of-a-kind in the world. On my first visit there, I was absolutely gobsmacked. "Whao! What a store," were the first words from my mouth. I can very well remember that the only items a person couldn't purchase from that store were cars and houses, even though there is a Harrods' estate agent and car showroom just down the road.

Be it intercontinental dishes, snacks, groceries, drinks, desserts, shoes, bags, accessories, men's and women's clothing, jewellery, electrical items, cosmetics, or anything else a person can think of, it's right there. All a person has to do is pay the stupendous prices attached to them.

For shopaholics, Oxford Street is the best place to be for all their clothing or shoe raves. I'm talking to the ladies here: it's a notably long, alive, and busy street where you are allowed to shop till you drop! The only problem one encounters on Oxford Street is knowing which of the shops to walk into.

OTHER TOURIST ATTRACTIONS

As great as tourism is in London, there are a myriad of other exciting and interesting places to visit in the UK. Starting with the Yorkshire region, the Yorkshire dales and moors are popular among tourists. Coupled with the cottages and farms around the West Yorkshire dales in places like Keighley, Ilkley, and Saltire Mills, various abbeys, like the Bolton abbey, are nearby.

Bradford has the Alhambra Theatre, the Museum of Colour and Photography, and Little Germany, the remains of the German architecture constructed during an influx of Germans into the city many years ago. The picturesqueness of the countryside and the moors in West Yorkshire provides opportunities to move away from the hustle-bustle of city life into solitude and some quiet.

York, one of the main tourist cities in the UK, is also situated in Yorkshire. With its castles and abbeys, York Cathedral, and the remains from when the Roman Empire conquered the city, York has a variety of attractions to offer any keen tourist.

In the midlands are Warwick Castle in Warwick, the Alton Towers theme park in Stoke-on-Trent, and not-to-be-missed Stratford-upon-Avon, Shakespeare's home town. For those who enjoy walking and climbing, the hilly Peak District and Lake District promise adventurous moments.

I utilised the few opportunities I had for tourism as a student. I guess it would be pointless to live in a foreign country and not tour its nooks and crannies as much as I could. All the trips were well worth it and were good values for money and time.

Good enough, the international office at my university organised many sight-seeing and day-out trips to various tourist places in the UK, choosing a day for an international students' trip once a month. Going in a group cut down the cost of travel and offered excellent company for many of us. These trips were relatively cheaper than going by public transport or in the company of few friends. It was always relaxing to travel out of the university area to see other parts of the country.

෧ఌ

CHAPTER 4
GENERAL SHOPPING TIPS MAKING MONEY WORK HARDER

Students are generally considered to be skint but I have noticed that is not always a true assumption. You'd be surprised to see students walk into a restaurant and have a nice steak meal and a bottle of wine to wash it down. Students might not have all the money in the world, but knowing how to economise, where to get the best bargains, and how to make the little available cash go farther is always key to living a great student life. Any student who learns to get the best deals in the market should be able to survive on more than baked beans and toast, the typical student meal.

For basic groceries, the big names like ASDA, Tesco, Morrisons, and Sainsbury's offer a wide variety of items. We could actually buy our writing materials, food, electronics, films, and basic amenities in the big stores. Most of them have buy-one-get-one-free offers, which someone like me got hooked on.

Morrisons supermarket, which seemed to have higher visibility in Bradford than most of the other big names, seemed to be the best at offering buy-one-get-one-free deals. Of course, if I wasn't careful, I could have ended up wasting my funds on items I didn't necessarily budget for just because I could buy one and get the other free.

Stores like ALDI, Netto, and Lidl offer bottom prices for a number of their items. Those stores were highly popular on my campus among us students. Funnily enough, there are some social stigmas attached to shopping in these cheap, bottom-price food shops. Some people believe that only low-class people shop in Lidl and Netto, and would not walk into them, lest their friends find out that they've been shopping from the bargain stores.

It was common to see students shop in Netto but bag the items in a Sainsbury's or Waitrose carrier bag. Who cares where people shop as long as they get good value for their hard-working money?

Another fabulous shop which I enjoyed is the Pound shop, or Poundland. Every item in the store, be it household utensils, food items, toiletries, or toys, costs only a pound. Of course, the social stigma of carrying a Poundland carrier bag on the street still holds for those who are concerned about their shopping image.

The other wonderful deals for students are the student discounts based on showing our student cards. That is if a student's university students' union is a member of the National Union of Students (NUS). Shops that offer the ten-to-twenty percent student discount would advertise by saying "NUS discounts available". NUS is inscribed at the back of each student card as proof of eligibility for discounts.

It is up to students to make enquires if stores offer the NUS discount. The interesting thing about the UK is that even though offers are available to people, if they are oblivious to them they might never get notified unless they ask. Asking from the student union office what offers or bargains we are entitled to as students is a good place to start. Always ask and ask and again, ask!

In addition to supermarkets, various cafes, restaurants, eateries, galleries, and cinemas offer student discounts, which one has to make enquiries about. The Cineworld cinemas in Bradford gave special rates to students on certain days of the week. Utilising all these avenues would make the pound stretch farther for any money-wise student.

DISCOUNT & STORE CARDS

For someone like me who didn't have a lot of money flowing in, using discount cards was another avenue for making my money work harder. Stores like Tesco supermarkets give club cards which earn their holders points for every pound spent in their stores. There is also the Nectar card from Sainsburys, and Morissons has a card as well. The idea behind these cards is to spend more in their stores and get rewarded for undivided loyalty to them. A chain of stores like Tesco offers gift vouchers for a certain number of points earned.

Another card I got wind of was the BiTE card, which gives me twenty percent off foods and drinks in all UK train stations. Then there is the 16-25 rail card which offers one-third off all rails fares for anyone in full-time education in the country. Irrespective of age, as long as a person is in full time education, that person is entitled to the railcard, which is obviously not free. Nothing is really free in the UK. If it advertised free, delving a bit deeper shows that there is a price attached to it. Students pay a tiny amount for the card, but it means that they can save an awful lot of money throughout the year on rail travels.

Add the National Express discount coach card to the list and I had some extra at my disposal. Like the rail card, the coach card goes for a few pounds, which can be easily gained back from the journeys made. All these offers being given to students shows how the UK system encourages individuals to pursue higher education.

If only incentives like these were to be put in place in the African systems, it would make it easier to study without tears. In spite of the system's rough edges, it's heartening to see how many African students strive to gain education, not minding the odds. Paradoxically, many young Britons complain about not being supported enough to gain the university educations they desire.

However, store cards, which are more like credit cards, should be avoided unless extreme circumstances warrant their use. They entice students by offering interest-free credit for a set period of time on items purchased from the store. The interest-free period can be as long as six months, but the interest rate afterwards can be as high as twenty-nine percent. I see store cards and the incentives given when one signs up for them as baits for hooking their targets. Before individuals know what is going on, they can be hooked on credit cards and loans for a long time.

It's fine to get the store cards if you're disciplined enough to pay within the short space of interest-free time, but getting into the red is a terrible situation for students to be in, risking bailiff's letters through their letter boxes and court injunctions for defaulting on store card payments.

CHAPTER 5

WINE AND DINE CULTURE: EATING IN AND OUT

If there is an aspect of British life that I have enormously enjoyed, it is the wine-and-dine culture. Be it in supermarkets, take-away outlets, or restaurants, a wide variety of different menus and choices are available.

Chinese and Thai food, sushi, Indian and Kashmiri curries, Caribbean jerk chicken and curry goat, Creole Jambalaya, and sumptuous African dishes are all readily accessible, not to mention Mediterranean food, Italian pizzas, Italian risottos. Moroccan couscous, English roasts and pies, Irish potato-based meals, and Mexican enchiladas and fajitas. The eating choices I could avail myself to were almost innumerable.

Being of West African origin, where home-cooked meals are considered priceless, I wasn't used to this eating-out culture. I could consider eating out on a few odd occasions, but those were for special times or in the company of friends. Interestingly, I noticed that Brits see eating out and having take-away meals as the order of the day. No wonder there are so many restaurants with huge annual turnovers in the country. If it was left to people like me, I doubt if the restaurants would make enough to make ends meet.

The first introduction I had to foreign foods was on the day of my arrival in Leeds. My cousin Ola, who picked me from the coach station, asked me what I wanted to eat. His options seemed weird to me.

He started by saying, "I'm sure you are hungry and you can have any food you like. You've got lasagna, chicken curry, chicken pies, and some pasta in the freezer."

I looked at him in shock, trying to understand what those weird things were.

After a few minutes, I went to him quietly and said, "Brother Ola, please, have you not got proper food at home?"

I was expecting him to offer me vegetable soup with eba or pounded yam, or better still, rice and stew. How did he expect me to eat all those strange items he considered to be food? That evening, I was forced to eat bread with stew since I was still familiar with that. The next day he bought the ingredients from the African shop to cook me what I considered real meals.

Ready-made microwave and oven meals are a big part of British culture. Even though I admire Brits' adventurous attitude to intercontinental dishes, I found it difficult to understand why people couldn't cook their meals from scratch and save money. I reckon that when it comes to food, Brits go for the idea that variety is the spice of life. They eat any kind of food as long as it is edible and eaten by some other people.

I remember how hesitant I was to try a meal of chicken curry the first time I was offered one. On another occasion I was offered lasagna al fonte and I still considered it to be less than real food, real food to me being an African dish of rice with plantain and properly cooked meat or fish stew, not this funny stuff I was being offered.

A few years down the line I have been miraculously transformed into the intercontinental cuisine lady, whose taste buds have finally adapted to dishes from around the globe. Blame it all on my adventurous British friends and work colleagues. They successfully got my taste buds and appetite transformed into what they have become now, not that they ever stuffed food down my throat in the process, though.

It's almost unbelievable how I now devour pasta, Bolognese, risottos, enchiladas, fajitas, naan bread, chapatti, poppadums, jacket potatoes with cheese filling, chow mein, black bean sauce, sweet and sour chicken, Jamaican jerk chicken, rice and peas, dumplings, sausage and mash potato, steak with roast potatoes and vegetables, stir fries, bread and soup, and of course the traditional British fish and chips with mushy peas.

The first time I told a Nigerian aunt that I take soup and bread for lunch, she looked at me with such pity and asked me why I had decided to starve myself. The look she gave me could have been interpreted that she had just heard a revealed mystery from me. Quick and simple meals like hot soup and crusty bread are time-savers and great for student survival.

At first, I never ceased to wonder why British food revolved basically around potatoes and bread. Toast is the main deal for breakfast, either with a bowl of cereal or eggs. For lunch it's still bread, but with fillings. Then for dinner it could still be soup and bread or a cooked pie.

Even though bread constitutes a typical quick breakfast, a traditional English breakfast is usually large and sumptuous, with butter or marmalade on toast, baked beans, grilled mushrooms and tomatoes, bacon, fried, scrambled, or poached eggs, fried bread, sausages, and black pudding. Such a breakfast would not be complete without a bowl of cereal and a cup of tea to wash it down.

Black pudding, which looks like sausage, is dark in colour and is made from dried pigs' blood and fat. Hmm! Yuck! It differs from region to region, with some being more peppery and fatty than others. Since the day I was told what black pudding is made of, I chose to avoid it whenever I get the chance to have a full English breakfast.

I was still fascinated with bread and the different forms in which it appears. Irrespective of the names given to the types, I still consider them to be bread. Be it French croissants, bagels, waffles, tortilla wraps, crumpets, sliced bread and malted loaf, Panini, or baguettes.

The preparation of a traditional English breakfast is so time consuming that students' traditional breakfast is baked beans on toast. Any student who is properly baptised into the system has baked beans on toast as his or her favourite delicacy in no time. It seems like the cereal packs and baked beans tins are all that's left when students run out of most grocery items. It's just the way it works.

Aside from the Sunday roast meal of beef, pork, gammon, lamb, or chicken with potatoes and vegetables, sandwiches are commonly the preferred lunchtime meal. The first time I saw able-bodied adults having those tiny sandwiches for lunch, I couldn't but wonder how they ever got sustained and filled up. Interestingly, I discovered that a number of accompaniments, like fruits, crisps, nuts, and biscuits, go with the bread. Oh! Sorry, I meant to say sandwich. As far as I am concerned, it's just bread and nothing more.

Another quickie for students, which as a fresher I considered acceptable, was take-away chicken and chips. It's not only quick, but also within an average student's budget. A lunch of kebab on naan bread or with chips is another quick students' lunch. I was still converting what things cost into Nigerian currency, so after spending so much on lunch daily I decided to choose the cheapest option of having my own packed lunch. As long as it didn't require microwaving during the day, it was convenient and handy. At the end of the day I could eat a healthier meal, since I knew what was in the food and at the same time save up a few quid.

Before we get on with lunch, I was surprised to learn that in certain parts of England, the afternoon meal I refer to as lunch is called dinner and they refer to the evening meal as tea. Prior to hearing of an evening meal being tea, I always thought of it as either dinner or supper. The whole concept was confusing to me at first.

A particular classmate of mine brought my attention to these new terms for meal times when she asked me to leave the lecture hall with her for dinner. Dinner? At 12.30 noon? I played along with her thinking that she was only pulling my legs, only for her to notify another classmate of ours that we were off for dinner in the students' refectory.

By this time, I was fully convinced that she was making a sincere mistake and sought to correct her by telling her that it was lunchtime, being in the afternoon, and not dinnertime. She was a native of Bradford and insisted that it was dinner and not lunch. Confused, I decided to ask the lecturer who came into the lecture hall after the lunch period. He laughed it off and explained to me that the mix-up was a northern-southern divide issue. Lunch is the word down South in London.

What another informative and educative session I had with that clarification. How do I explain that someone is eating his tea? The whole mix-up still sounds funny to me whenever I consider it. In case you are wondering, I now eat dinner in the afternoon and tea in the evening. Interesting idea, eh?

In most cases, British lunch is usually light and supper is a cooked meal. Most times, the cooked meals would be casseroles and pies. They could be fish pie, chicken pie, meat pie, cottage pie, steak and ale pie, or vegetable pie. Any kind of pie can be encountered in British meals, even some combinations of pies I had never heard of.

By the end of the three years at university, I had eaten virtually every dish available in England and I was enjoying them all. It was almost unbelievable that I, who was once extremely reserved about trying new dishes, could devour most meals as long as they were palatable.

CHAPTER 6

REAL STUDENT LIFE

One thing that never ceases to fascinate me about the UK system of education is the well-structured and organised way by which it works. Times and events are well programmed without fail at the beginning of each session. From the outset, students are informed of the module timetables, tutorials, coursework and assignment-submission deadlines, exam periods, laboratory times, and all that they really need to know.

For someone like me who came from a different style of university education, one which wasn't privileged to have this level of organisation, it seemed impossible and unbelievable. I thought to myself that they would not follow all those set-out plans to the letter, only to be dismayed that the system was actually run as laid down. One of these was the university orientation week. I had just arrived from Nigeria and had decided to give myself a few days break before going to lectures while I sorted out my student registration and departmental familiarisation. What a mistake I made doing that!

I paid the price for that single week of lectures that I missed well during the semester, as I had a huge pile of lecture notes to be attended to afterwards. The kindness of some gracious classmates saw me through this trying period of my settling down into university.

Now, here is the deal for students who are going to attend a British university: if a date is fixed for orientation and welcoming there, they need to make sure they avail themselves of that opportunity at the time stated, because those dates will be religiously adhered to. I discovered that British universities usually play by the rules and try not to cut corners, since the consequences of doing so might be too costly.

Even though the time lost had its toll on me, the academic staff did their best to salvage the situation I was in. I was given review lectures and tutorials to catch up with the rest of the class and supplied with extra materials. In spite of all the synchronised organisation, the universities still make allowances for anomalies and see to the students' general welfare.

They always told us that the university runs because of the patronage of the students, who are therefore treated as customers, rather than the staff members declaring themselves as the supreme powers, as it is in some parts of the world. That was indeed breathtaking for me. Coming to terms with this took me a while, but I guess I got there in the end.

Let's face it, in reality that statement could not be too far from the truth, especially if one considers the financial input of international students into the university systems and the educational system as a whole. International student revenues alone inject billions of pounds into the UK economy.

With that knowledge, I fully agree with them that the students are the greatest assets to the smooth running of the universities, without running down the inestimable inputs of the academic and non-academic staff. As an international student, one might as well walk with the shoulder high and feel proud to be part of that highly priced input.

Yeah! The UK system still mesmerises me with how set life is for the average student. Many support mechanisms were there to help us settle down well into the academic system, the hall life, social events, the student union, university library, internet access and use, and all that goes with it.

I had just started the second year of the biomedical science degree at the University of Bradford, West Yorkshire, having spent almost three years as an undergraduate in Nigeria. Even though I had read through the prospectus and the university brochures on academic and university life, I was badly prepared for what I met and got. Some of the promises in the prospectus seemed too good to be true, but on the whole most of them actually were true.

Here was I, as a new student in class on the first day, not knowing who to speak to and how to go about the day-to-day activities, even though the departmental office had provided such learning materials as the timetables, scheduled lecture halls, and the lecturers to take each module.

The one-week delay had a negative impact on my ability to settle down quickly and to familiarise myself with the lecturers, but a wonderful lady in the class named Becky came to my rescue. She offered me photocopies of some of the printed notes and even copied some of her handwritten notes for me, mentioned the individual lecturers, and introduced me to some of our fellow students.

I had a great first-hand experience of the British courtesy and politeness which I had read of prior to my arrival, although some of the horrible experiences I had afterwards almost made nullified this.

Nonetheless, they say first impressions last long, and the first kindness I experienced shaped my perception throughout my university days. Generally speaking, the people tended to be polite, even though I came to understand later that it might have been guarded politeness or political correctness that motivated such courtesy.

So, to my new-found friend I thought that if someone went out of her way as she did, it meant that she wanted to foster a good friendship and classmate relationship, but then I met one of the greatest culture shocks that were in store for me. I tried speaking to her a number of times after classes, just to be an acquaintance, if anything for the invaluable assistance she willingly offered me in my first weeks. It was strange to me that her attitude was a bit cold. I thought maybe it was just the reserved British nature, but to my utmost surprise an offer I made to buy her coffee during our break time and maybe get to know her was plainly turned down for no reason.

Even though she did refuse my company and friendliness, she still tried to help me with any challenging situation in the lecture halls. What strange and paradoxical behaviour! Being African and brought up not to refuse kind gestures from people without a definite reason, I found the whole situation embarrassing and a bit frustrating. I thought that one good thought deserved another, but certainly not in this case. How on earth could anyone explain how someone can smile so brightly and chat so exuberantly in the lecture hall, but act like a total stranger once we stepped out of that hall, as if we had never met before in our lives?

This was a big and indelible lesson I got. As I later gathered from the native Britons who became my friends as the years went by, that could be the typical behaviour of an average Brit. It's nothing personal at all, but as they put it, "An average British person has many boxes and compartments." It's also said that a British man doesn't trust you until he trusts you. I came to understand this more clearly by experience. It means that I could walk into a pub or restaurant with someone here, have a great chat and get to know each other without that person considering me to be a friend or me considering myself to be one.

We could belong to the same sports team at university and get on well together during our practices and matches, but when we meet in a café we only get to be familiar strangers, or at worst total strangers. I mean, this drove home the point that I was indeed in a different world – the Western world. At first, this attitude came across as mind-boggling, as many questions raced down my heart. Is this the way foreigners are treated? Is it an individual's personality? Has this got something to do with me? A combination of all these questions raced through my mind.

As an international student, I realised that the way foreigners are perceived could be puzzlingly funny. People who have not had any contacts or close relationships with those from other continents are usually misinformed about who they are and where they're from. All many mostly know about Africa is that it has extreme famine, poverty, suffering, and malnutrition. Unfortunately, some based the way they related to me on these perceptions.

A classmate of mine was so curious to know about the African continent that he asked me a thousand and one questions about the whole of Africa and the "practices and traditions" people there lived by. I initially thought that he was just being inquisitive until he asked me some bewildering questions. He asked first if I was African, to which I answered in the positive. He then asked if it was true that we all lived in mud-thatched houses and went hunting for animals to eat for our daily sustenance, if we wore proper clothes, and if we actually had proper educational institutions.

Believe me, I was not only shocked and startled at his ignorance of how things operate in various continents in the twenty-first century, but also lost for words. In the true spirit of being a bonafide Nigerian, I answered those questions with other questions. That's just the way we are. To get him reasoning a bit at least, I asked how he thought I fitted into the educational system, having been admitted into the second year of the course rather than the first, if the so-called third-world countries provided no educational foundation.

In response to his questions about clothes, shelter, and animal hunting, I tried explaining a bit, then pointed him in the right direction to get geography books and other materials that would make him better educated. Oh! You won't believe that someone who was born and bred in a country like the UK would lack access to first-class information and geographical knowledge about the rest of the world.

Another African friend of mine had a similar experience, in which he was asked by a course mate if people wear shoes in his country or walk around barefooted. These and many more embarrassing, sometimes amusing and irritating questioning sessions I faced introduced me to the UK system.

Okay, let me answer some of those questions. Yes, we Africans live as families in trees, kill live wildlife with spears, arrows, and in some cases barehanded. We eat food raw and walk barefooted. We know not what electricity is and have no television or satellite systems, but yes, we jump off those trees, go to school by hopping from tree to tree, get certifications, apply to UK universities, and jump on the plane – all of this naked, of course! Isn't that a stimulating and interesting approach to life?

I know well that international students from other parts of the world received even worse questions, posed by some well-educated ignoramuses. I guess they're part of the system. As an international student, we shouldn't be too shocked to hear them or be too irritated to give tutorials and lectures on how things work in our homelands. Welcome on board to the journey of an international student in the UK.

LECTURES AND MODULES

The moment the university session began was the same time that we got started with lectures. Even tutorial class organised by lecturers and doctorate researchers that were part of the timetable commenced right away. Back in Nigeria, the first weeks would be used for nothing other than settling down, registering for different courses, and other informal activities.

At the beginning of each session and semester we were required to register at our departments and for the courses and modules we'd be taking that session. The timetable, summary of the lectures for each module, practical notebooks, list of textbooks and materials needed, and the laboratory coats were handed over to each student. Knowing what we were up to academically prepared me for the journey ahead, but it was strangely too structured to come to terms with easily.

My first weeks at lectures were a bit challenging because of the layout and patterns. Beautifully, the class was not too large, typical of UK universities, with about forty to sixty students. That meant that the lecturers had access to each student and knew when we were away from a class. By the time I was in my final year, the attendance register were taken for all the classes because the authorities wanted to ensure that we took our academics and classes seriously.

Being a new student meant that I usually sat in the first two rows and listened to the lecturers with rapt attention. That wasn't just because I was a dedicated student, but because understanding the different lecturers' different British accents was difficult for me. I remember asking a classmate of mine what language a particular lecturer spoke because I couldn't fully comprehend what he was saying. It turned out that he was speaking English, but being a Canadian he had a totally different accent.

The Yorkshire accent on its own is a different kettle of fish, and I had to listen ardently to understand people. The speed at which some of them spoke, which as a Nigerian with a totally different English accent I wasn't used to, made understanding them difficult.

I had thought that the easily understood Queen's English accent was spoken throughout UK, but I faced this variety of accents instead.

Only two of us in the class were Africans, and we had two Chinese international students as well. All the others were home students who didn't have to face the communication challenges that we did. A friend of mine who had initially faced the challenge of understanding the lecturers clearly took a tape recorder into the class to record all the lectures, which she listened to afterwards. With time, she overcame the communication barrier and was fine. That was an option, though the lecturers often went out of their way with visual teaching aids and lecture notes to ensure smooth communication and understanding of what they were saying.

I realised that Bradford uses the modular system for each subject. This means that every subject taken as a module for a semester stands on its own and is not an addendum to the next module or subject. At my previous university back in Nigeria, which used the course system, a course could sometimes be a continuation of a course taken the previous semester, which means that Biology 102 in the second semester would normally be a continuation of Biology 101 taken in the first semester.

On the other hand, with the modular system, all the modules are always relevant, but each concentrates only on the knowledge of that core area and is covered in detail during that period. As many advantages as the course system has, I personally prefer the modular system, because if a module was not my strong area, once I was through with it that semester I could drop it and get to focus on my strong areas.

As biomedical science students, we were required to have practical classes most days of the week. That was relatively tiring and demanding. The only exceptions were some Wednesdays, when all universities are required to finish academic work by 1.00 pm for students' sporting and extra-curricular activities.

That was different to what I knew before, because no part of the Nigerian university system gave us time for such activities. I felt that it was too much to spend two to three hours every day in a laboratory, but come to think of it, the main essence of the education wasn't just to gain the theoretical knowledge but to be able to put the knowledge into practice and to work. How better could one demonstrate the knowledge without getting the practical skills? I adjusted as fast as I could to this mode of education, even though the pace seemed to be racing.

Inside the laboratory was another experience on its own. Well equipped and staffed for the students, learning to use this sophisticated equipment was another hurdle for me to overcome. You could ask me a lot of questions about the analyses and methods in use theoretically and I'd give you the answers up front, but having hands-on experience was another issue altogether. There I was, having been used to mouth pipettes, at the University of Bradford which only used calibrated and programmed pipettes.

To my utter dismay, most of the equipment I had used in Nigeria was obsolete in the scientific world. Internationally recognised institutes are moving with the times and technological advancements, and I was faced with no choice than to get compliant. Most of my classmates had no idea that I couldn't figure out how to operate this equipment. I didn't hesitate to inform the lecturer in charge quietly that I needed help. He and the laboratory technicians were more than helpful in saving me from a lot of embarrassment. God bless them for bailing me out. Who knows if I would have become the laughing stock of the class.

Since every student had her or his own desk and equipment in the laboratory, feigning the skills to my fellow students was not a difficulty, and in no time I had mastered the main things and was willing to lend a helping hand to whoever needed it in the class.

Whenever we had to work in groups as well, I always volunteered to carry out the practical aspects of the experiments while someone else did the result recordings and other aspects of the tasks. I am sure many of my mates thought I was just being enthusiastic and dedicated to the tasks. If only they knew that it was my secret strategy for building confidence in using this complex equipment and to gain the skills for using it effectively. One always has to find his or her way around issues in life, you know. The most important thing was that I created my own wave and caught up with the technology.

Classes were going on fine and I settled well into the system. My understanding of the different accents improved with time as well. An aspect that I really enjoyed with the teaching was the use of such visual aids as posters or pictures and most of the lecture notes being normally presented on MS PowerPoint delivered via a projection screen. All we had to do as students was to take notes on the important bits of lectures rather than having to take whole lectures down in writing – definitely simpler.

ACADEMIC SUPPORT, TUTORIALS, AND PERSONAL TUTORS

As I mentioned, the academic and non academic members of staff were always there to help, but thare wasn't a daily one-to-one tuition, as some people are made to believe. The system is great, but I doubt if one-to-one tuition is feasible in a higher educational institution. A few times that I had issues with the lectures and unfamiliar modules, I got all the help I needed from the staff, ranging from additional notes to simple explanations or even scheduled slots for expatiating the topics. Not a bad deal, eh?

Tutorial classes organised by some lecturers and doctorate research students were some of the academic support mechanisms that we received. The tutorials that I was used to in my previous university had been organised by the academic staff but delivered by students in a higher class of the same course. If, for example, someone was a first-year pharmacy student, that student's tutorial classes would be moderated and facilitated by either a third or fourth-year student. That way it was more of an interactive session between students and would not be a part of the timetable, being organised rather informally in the students' spare time.

It was a bit of a surprise to me that in Bradford University the tutorials are scheduled into the timetable and are not optional. The tutorial sessions are a must for receiving the maximal output from the academy, and are extremely useful, too. The most important tutorials are the examination revision sessions. I can't tell you how useful those were, especially when the lecturers in charge conducted them.

They provided a number of tips on how to study and revise for the examination papers for those who are smart enough to decipher and read in between the lines of what they say. Those sessions were keenly interesting, because all of a sudden students who weren't otherwise keen in class became the most enthusiastic and interested. Something that I learnt was that by listening closely to what the lecturers said at this time I knew the areas to concentrate my revision efforts on, and that paid off reasonably well.

PERSONAL TUTORS

A particularly important support mechanism we had as students was having an assigned personal tutor. On entering the department, I was informed of which lecturer was my personal tutor. Having not had that before and being unfamiliar with the system, I didn't know fully what her role was to me. The university timetable had designated times throughout the session to meet up with this personal tutor. Her role wasn't to give lectures or elucidate on topics from classes, but to serve as a university guardian, or adopted parent.

My first meeting with my personal tutor was relaxed and totally informal, as were all our other meetings. I couldn't come to terms with what in my opinion was the too-friendly approach with which she related to me. She asked me personal questions about my previous university and about how I was settling down, such as where I lived, how I commuted to university, whether the lectures were going down well, and many other personal things. As I settled more into the system,

I realised that the position of my personal tutor was that of someone I could talk to about any situation that affected my studies, and that meant anything. As long as I was comfortable with it, that is considered part of my personal tutor's job.

Considering that I was used to an impersonal relationship with lecturers, I didn't quite utilise the abilities of my personal tutor as much as I should have at the onset. In Nigeria, the lecturers are the mighty lords, and we the students were vassals at their mercies. Even if we ever had the chance to meet some of these really horrible lecturers, we'd avoid them, lest we get into any trouble they might cook up.

Over here in the UK, fellow students contacted their personal tutors when they had ill-health that could potentially affect their studies, when they had family or domestic issues, or even money problems. That's not to mean that personal tutors are fairy godparents, but they'd suggest ways to cope, recommend any help or support the university or department offered, and might even intervene in extending coursework deadlines if the need be.

When I got my first part-time job in Bradford, my personal tutor stood in as a referee to the recruitment agency, although the agency staff were reluctant to accept the reference, considering that my tutor had known me for barely five months at the time. I had to seek another referee who had known me for a number of years prior to my resumption at university. As time went on, though, I continually used her as my referee and even for some posts I applied for after university.

Once I thought I was already in trouble with her when I stood with some classmates in the corridor to her office mimicking her and acting out the way she talked in class. I had barely finished my mischievous act when she walked past and said a lovely hello to all of us. She never mentioned it, but I'm looking forward to her asking me when she gets around to reading this. Students will always be students, won't they – naughty and ever mischievous.

It wasn't unusual to pop into my tutor's office just to catch up with her on what was happening to me and how I was coping with the heavy academic workload, my social life, and my part-time job. The few times that she wasn't too busy she would offer me a cup of tea and some biscuits. How better could I unwind after some laborious laboratory session?

There were also times that she continually rescheduled meetings with me week after week until I got tired of running after her. All that was part of student life and I had to live with it. Honestly, the importance of a personal tutor and the efficient utilisation of that support system cannot be overemphasised, especially for an international student who might not know the ways around UK student life.

MEET SOME OF MY LECTURERS

My lecturers were fantastic people on the whole, but individually they were interesting characters. Some of them were stimulating, while others bored the lives out of us in class. I had some who would not complain about a thing and some who wouldn't take nonsense from anyone.

My personal tutor, Dr Gaynor, was a character on her own, both down-to-earth and strict. No messing around with her. Everyone knew that when it was her class, they had to have their best foot forward. She didn't seem to care in the least way what anyone thought of her, but she did a great job straightening people up in class. Honestly, without someone like her, the class would have gone haywire a lot of times. She knew how to sort students out excellently. Funnily enough, she was most accommodating as a personal tutor, but please, can I describe her as a workaholic?

Many a time I'd get out of the hall late in the evening and she'd just be leaving her office building. Once I walked up to her and asked why she stayed this late at uni. She just explained that she was dealing with work until 8 pm. It was none of my business, anyway, but no wonder she gave us loads of assignments and calculations which I so much loathed. At the end of the day, I only got better for it. Another striking thing about her was her Scottish accent, which was a bit fun to me. At least, I had the chance to listen to another accent rather than the everyday Yorkshire one.

The head of department, Dr Dawson, was just like a mother to everyone in the department. If anyone had any problem, they could be well assured of her listening ears and compassion, even though a few students tried to take that for license. They had this impression that she was gullible and tried playing many tricks on her. If a coursework was due and someone didn't want to hand it in at the stipulated time, they'd walk up to her and tell her some well-cooked-up story, but more often than not they got a wonderfully kind and soft response with a wonderful NO.

I once tried it, too, when some of my mates told me to speak to her to get a time extension to the submission of my coursework. I told her that I was just stressed up few days to the submission and would appreciate it if I could get more time, stress in this case meaning dealing with other things and allowing them to take my precious time. The answer was soft but firm. "Sorry, the deadline has to be adhered to." Of course, I eventually submitted it in the nick of time, but was only pushing my luck with the HOD.

You don't want to know that one of our lecturers was nicknamed Father Xmas. He was this big, tall, and heavily built man with grey hair and moustache. That earned him the well-deserved name and title. Prof, a highly intelligent and outstandingly brilliant man, was an icon in his field and was well travelled. He'd come to class to tell us of his journeys and trips, which almost sounded that no work was involved other than the fun of sight-seeing and travelling. His work took him as far as the Middle East, USA, Europe, and anywhere you could imagine. At times I envied him with all these trips, and requested to be taken along once. Unfortunately, the time and resources weren't available until he retired.

Guess what his major interest of discussion in class was besides academic issues? His wife. He would rave about his wife, her work and accomplishments in class to no end. I used to wonder what the issue was with the man and why he felt we needed to know his wife, only to discover that his wife was a world-renowned dermatologist and researcher. No wonder he went on about her. Who wouldn't, anyway?

Even though I wasn't privileged to be a student directly under her, I knew her from a distance. A glimpse of her told you that she was living up to the standards as a dermatologist. Inspite of her age, her skin looked marvellously beautiful and youthful. She was a great advertisement for her area of expertise.

I had another interesting lecturer who later became a good acquaintance of mine after I told him of my career plans. He was greatly encouraging and challenged me to go all the way for it. As wonderful as he was as a person, I almost got fed up of him in class. He was undertaking some studies on some tumour suppressors at the time, so any topic he lectured on related back to this particular tumour suppressor gene.

In no time, his students had nicknamed him The Gene. It seemed like the thoughts of that area had him completely obsessed. Even when I met him in his office he would drift from the topic to his research area. That didn't encourage me to consider being a researcher; maybe my whole world would basically revolve around a concept known only to me and my academic folks.

One lecturer who caught my attention in the final year was Dr Thompson, who was remarkably gentle and could handle no hassles. She was extremely feminine and spoke so softly that some students would try to disturb her classes at every chance. She was also really feminine and classy with her dressing. I really liked her fashion sense, since not many lecturers in the department dress fashionably. She was always wearing her stiletto heels and skirts or dresses — a classic example of being a lady.

Once I told her this and she said a wonderful thank you in her usual gentle way. I reckon my liking her as a person affected my performance in the course she lectured. I had a distinction in that particular course. She was the lady in the department. Her approach to academics made me realise that being an academic could still avail me the chance to have a great sense of fashion and time to attend to myself.

One lecturer I would forever remember was the statistics lecturer who taught us in the final year how to analyse experimental data using the SPSS programme. He got the nickname of Cuckoo Eggs because he used cuckoo eggs as examples in all his explanations and designs. I hardly understood his cuckoo eggs theory, but he at least got us interested and entertained with chickens and birds laying cuckoo eggs. What on earth cuckoo eggs had to do with data analysis is totally beyond me.

The mix of various lecturers, their styles, and approaches showed how one could fit into academia and not get boxed up into certain stereotypes. Some whose only focus was academics would give an impression that being a lecturer meant being deep and sometimes boring, while the lively ones gave the impression of having a great career and a life in return.

♋

CHAPTER 7
STUDYING HARD OR SMART?

If you are like me, you might have heard statements like, "Studying in UK is dead easy." Those of us from Nigeria were told that studying abroad is much easier than anywhere else, that the standards of education are falling generally, and that education in the UK is more about socials and fun. Believe me, I had heard all those phrases and then some before I came over to university in the UK. I was made to believe that passing examinations would be an easy stride, only to be faced with the truth right in my face. It wasn't!

In reality, a high number of students party, binge-drink, and go a-clubbing on a regular and consistent basis, but that is not because the educational standards or the course curricula are downgraded in any way. I was absolutely shocked because I thought that the amount of effort I had to put into my academic work would be minimal as long as I attended all the lectures. The truth was that the two weeks of lecture that I missed at the start of the term, coupled with my integration into the system as a fresher, had a massively adverse effect on my performance for the first semester. Piling up lecture notes had its own negative effect as well. The reason, as I noticed, is that the modular system works in such a way that students need to cover every area of that course in order to get average marks in that module.

The assessments of the modules were such that we needed to study as many as three or four certain areas of the subject for the coursework for a single module. In addition to coursework, we were expected to carry out group discussions and presentations, and in some cases make out topical posters which we presented to the whole class.

To make matters more interesting, for some of the group works each member of the group would be asked to suggest a mark for every other member of the group based on individual performances in carrying out the task. In effect, each student would assess the other students in the group anonymously. Bearing that in mind spurred everyone in the group into action, making the likelihood of being an active group member higher.

Despite that, there were still some irresponsible students who cared less about group work or academic issues in general. To make matters worse, my hall mates in my first year went out clubbing at least three nights a week, excluding weekends. The impression their attitudes presented to me was that we could take academic matters easy and still be fine.

They considered people like me, who visited the library consistently out of normal university opening hours of 9 am to 5 pm, to be bookworms. It was no surprise to me that a number of them graduated with third-class degree classifications or ordinary passes. I doubt if any international student in his or her right senses could afford to graduate with those degree classes, considering the amount of resources invested into this type of education. That is not to mean that all the social butterflies and party animals were at the bottom of the classes all the same.

Some students that I knew enjoyed their partying and effectively balanced that with their academic commitments. I believe moderation is the word here for a healthy social and academic life. The old adage that all work and no play makes Jack a dull boy can be adopted to get a balance of both. However, all play and no work would make Jack a big-time idiot, too.

Throughout any academic session, it was usually a case of *ready, steady, go*, because we hardly had respite in between coursework, scheduled tests, seminars, case-study presentations, and examinations. A number of international students like me, mainly fellow Nigerians, lamented endlessly about the misrepresentation of the UK academic system. It was still okay for the undergraduates who could make amends in the second and third years, which are the only two academic sessions used for an undergraduate degree assessment anyway, but no fun for the masters students, who had only two semesters to bag their degrees.

By the end of the first semester, the masters students would be coming to terms with the heavy workload laden on them, and while they were recovering from that the second semester would have arrived with its own heavy baggage. Before you could say "Jack Robinson," the exams would have arrived and gone, with the students only to be left with the dissertation. I experienced so many postgraduate students angry at the presumption of a walk-through academic system which didn't only prove them wrong, but confronted them as a giant in the midst of their helplessness. The wise thing to do is not to start studies with a lackadaisical attitude. Putting in all our efforts from the outset is usually worth it every step of the way.

To be rightly said, UK education could prove to be highly demanding, yet ultimately fulfilling. Students graduate from the university with the confidence of being well-baked graduates, equipped with the knowledge and skills needed in the workplace. This is where I knowing that people don't just bag a degree, but painstakingly earn it. With all the challenging situations we were subjected to, graduating from the university had not only empowered me intellectually, but also socially, and with a wider perspective of life and the working of the global industry.

EXAMINATIONS, ASSESSMENTS, AND COURSEWORK

My first year at the University of Bradford was challenging. Settling down and understanding the whole academic system was a different ballgame altogether, especially since I was a second-year direct-entry student. Had I started in the first year, I guess I would have gathered the momentum for the journey and have been better prepared for the task ahead.

We were told that the results from the second year accounted for 30% of the whole degree qualification, while the final year's results took the remaining 70%. Interestingly, in all UK universities the results from the first year of an undergraduate degree do not count as part of the assessment for the award of the degree. Only the second and final years' results count.

This means that the first-year modules must be passed anyway to progress to the second year, but the main thing is obtaining a 40% mark to move on to the next year. If any course is failed in the first year,

a re-sit of the paper would take place and only on successful completion
of that does the student progress. That was a big shock to me because
in Nigeria every year and result counts and students have to pass all
their courses to progress and eventually graduate.

In the second year, 40% of the cumulative marks was awarded
from the coursework, which included tests, essay write-ups, and laboratory
practical write-up presentations, while examinations accounted for the
remaining 60%. That was a good arrangement, since the exams didn't
take up most of the marks. If one did not perform well with the
coursework, compensation could be easily achieved in the exams.

One mode of pre-examination assessment I personally
favoured was open-book tests. These involved taking in the laboratory
reports written after our practical classes. Instead of handing the write-
ups with the result interpretations to the lecturer in charge, we had
to use the laboratory results to answer the questions in the test. That
sounded a bit easy, but was in reality daunting. The times allocated to
such tests were so short that we needed to be able to interpret results
fast. Even though we were allowed our answer sheets as well, it had to be
our own practical work exclusively.

Students have a reputation for always trying to beat the system
and play fast games on the lecturers, and once a particular girl in my
class decided to play a fast game by using someone else's practical write-
up for answering test questions. The head of department (HOD), who
was one of the invigilators, decided to check to see that every student
was using his or her own write-up and discovered that the girl was
cheating by using someone else's. The HOD called the girls' attention to

what she had found out and announced out loud that she was cheating. She immediately took the write-up off the girl and instructed her to stand in front of the class.

To my utter dismay, the girl started struggling with the HOD for the sheets of paper, which were now in the latter's hand. Knowing fully well that her game was up, this girl became dramatic, in my opinion and recollection. She started screaming, "I've got a panic attack, and I need my doctor right away!" As she continually repeated these words, the whole class became disrupted as we watched the free drama scene going on in class. She was led out few minutes afterwards to seek medical help.

My goodness! Where on earth would any student get away with such behaviour, except of course in the UK? Panic attack, my foot! Even though she was taken away at that minute, how could we be sure she actually had a panic attack, other than that she was clearly covering up her misbehaviour. I was startled and surprised at the same time.

I could imagine if that student had been caught committing such a malpractice in Nigeria. She'd have had to pay the price shamefully, and no amount of panic attack would have saved her face. What lecturer would she even have had the guts to struggle with, or which one would listen to her panic-attack plea? Strangely, yet interestingly, this is the UK system, where health and human rights are considered paramount, irrespective of the offence committed, and given a higher priority.

Our course works had to be submitted at certain designated times, and we were often told to place them in the lecturers' pigeon holes. At first I didn't know what a pigeon hole was. "What on earth is that again?" I asked. Little did I know that they were the post boxes assigned to lecturers for any material that is to be handed over to them in their absence. You can imagine why it is called a pigeon hole and not something else. If the deadline for the coursework is 4 pm, any that came in after that time would be discredited because the issue of time limits and time keeping are serious and extremely weighty.

REVISION TIPS: UTILISING PAST EXAM-QUESTION PAPERS

Using past questions was absolutely invaluable as part of effective revision for exams. Past examination questions from two or three previous years were provided at the back of the module handbooks, but being a novice to the system I didn't know how helpful tackling these questions as part of my revision was. In all sincerity, most of my first semester exam questions were a repeat of the past questions. If only I had utilised them as efficient tools my results would have been much better than they turned out to be for those papers.

With the knowledge that most examination questions are usually from the past few years, I and a number of my classmates learnt to tackle the past questions, and that strategy worked wonders. The only snag about that is that we wouldn't know exactly which ones it would be, and if time was not greatly on our side while revising, having the past examination questions might not have helped much .

The smart thing we did was divide the previous years' questions amongst us in groups and for each individual to write out the main points and essays for each question. That way, we could have the answers to most of the questions without necessarily doing all the work personally. I'm sure that even the authorities would recognise our efforts as part of teamwork building. Still, much of the time students ignore the advice of lecturers in using past questions as a vital part of their revisions for exams.

That's not to mean that there couldn't be a downside to using past exam questions exclusively for revision. I remember a particular module for which I only earned a borderline pass because I focused too much on the past questions. It was the medical biochemistry module, in which the lecturer in charge overemphasised particular areas when talking about examination revision.

Taking that on board, I over-revised those areas and treated the past questions with ardent concentration, only to be faced with exam questions that did not examine that particular area. It wasn't a funny occurrence at all. Still, as long as one leaves no stone unturned, the revision tips should pay off.

Nevertheless, past exam questions are mostly a plus in preparing for examinations. However, we had to get the past questions from the library in the middle of the semester before the exams approached at all, lest other students got them first and didn't return them on time for others to use.

GLUED TO THE LIBRARY

Was I a bookworm? I suppose not, but I did enjoy every bit of my time in the library. I realised that most of university life revolved around the library. Without access to the library, being a student would be almost futile. Most of the lecture notes are placed on electronic blackboard, which is accessed via the university PCs located in the library, which also has group study rooms, a computer room, individual study rooms and cubicles, relevant textbooks, a backlog of major journals and research papers, and the photocopying machine.

My first day in the library was a memorable one for me. I was told that I needed my student identity card to gain entrance there and for any other transactions. On entering into the library, however, I noticed that no students had to show the security staff their student cards. Instead, all they had to do was to swipe the cards on a surface and the barricade opened. I followed suit as a JJC, and in no time I became conversant with the system. Whenever the swipe card did not work, access was denied and the student registry had to re-activate the card. No hanky-panky games here.

On that first day, I needed to get some books out of the library and I approached a staff member who advised me to use the self-service desk. Little did she know that I was unfamiliar with all this system's electronic tagging. As I tried to explain myself, she excused herself to attend to another person. I stood there with this bewildered and confused look, not knowing what to do immediately. Did I call someone to help me or go to the self-service desk to operate the PC?

With my totally confused self, I stood there momentarily only for a young lady to approach me. It was obvious that I was confused and needed help. She enquired if I was a new student and what could she do to help me. "Oh! This must be an angel," I muttered to myself. She'd arrived right in the nick of time. She put me through all the processes, which included the library registration and the PC registration, and explained everything that needed clarification to me. Fortunately, she was a fellow Nigerian student and later on became my closest friend on campus.

Now that I knew how to get around the library, I became glued to the place day and night. It was just fun browsing on the internet to no end and using all the materials at my disposal. The library was so well stuffed that the only problem I had was knowing which ones to choose. Good problem, eh? Chatting in the computer room was another enjoyable exercise. No wonder I met my closest friends at university in the library.

Even though I was mostly in the library, my aim wasn't to deal always with academic issues, as many of my classmates came to believe. If only they knew that I went in there mostly to use the internet and to read magazines in my leisure time. Many of them perceived me to be this academically inclined, studious student, and I was always bombarded with loads of questions on the modules and assignments we were given in class. Not that I was too far away from being that keenly studious student, but I doubt if I was truly that serious about academic work.

The library opened till late in the night, but later became open for twenty-four hours a day. That was a relief to nocturnal beings like me. Come exam periods, the place would be jammed like the market square with students reading their eyes out. We, the real consistent library customers, hardly had seats for our revision. By then we were more like the authorized club members who looked out for ourselves, reserving seats and PCs.

When it comes to students who can study without end, the Chinese students are hard to outdo. Their dedication to studying could be challenging and in some cases intimidating. They were there in the morning. Come noon I'd find them studying. They kept on studying even at night. I must have been hanging in there, too, or how else could I have noticed that?

Being stuck in the library had its own benefits for me. If nothing else, I enjoyed my moments there and came across as this deep and serious student – a geek maybe. I can imagine a number of students may have acted just like me, but were not as committed to studying their course materials as much as browsing on the computers. As great as my times were, I once had my mobile phone stolen from my cubicle while I excused myself to use the ladies' room. That was not funny at all. Students were supposed to be studying and revising hard in those few weeks before examinations, but some still had time for unscrupulous acts. You needed to see my sullen face that night as I left the library.

If the library authorities were fair, I should have been given a special identity number to signify my exuberant commitment and dedication to the place. In spite of not getting any recognition or award for being a great library user, I would still recommend that any student should utilise all the assets and materials in the library conscientiously.

❧

CHAPTER 8
IT'S A NEW WORLD: UNDERSTANDING PLAGIARISM

Here was I, a typical JJC from a Nigerian university, trying to find my feet at university in the UK, and I was being faced with some strange words, one of them being 'plagiarism'. It is classified as a grave university offence worthy of dismissal. "Really?" I asked myself. "Then it must be a seriously weighty issue that needs to be avoided by all means," I said. For crying out loud, with the vast amount of vocabulary in my custody, I simply hadn't heard of the word plagiarism and had to look it up in the dictionary.

Even if I was not merely interested in the meaning of the word, the penalty it carries, that the thousands of pounds paid by my parents could be go down the drain, propelled me into finding out. Expulsion from university was the last thing I could ever imagine. Imagine having to inform my parents of a crime known as plagiarism and that the fees are all gone. Anyway, I got the meaning at last. Thank God!

Plagiarism refers to any work a student submits or to which a student lays claim that is not original and with its author or other source not being credited. That's just my simple definition, and I feel it drives it home without much ado. All right then, I thought, it only meant not quoting the author of a journal article or paper in my write-up or essay, only to discover that writing down my classmate's definition of a phenomenon or writing down a mate's idea is also classified as plagiarism. That was a bit strange for me to comprehend at the time.

Even working in a group and using someone else's words or representing them as one's own is regarded as plagiarism. The most evident and common act of plagiarism is copying answers or information from the internet for academic purposes. I once heard of a student who was expelled from a university because most of his coursework assignments were basically downloaded from the internet. Worse still, his final-year project came from the same sources.

Sheer laziness, a nonchalant attitude, ignorance, or some combination of these might have been the reason or reasons. Whatever the reason was, plagiarism is a no-no. Lecturers claim they have plagiarism-detecting software in case any student wants to take the cheap way out. Since I stayed away from this heinous academic crime, I had no way to verify whether such software programmes are actually available to academics.

I stayed successfully away from plagiarism of any kind and graduated with a good honours degree. Other forms of plagiarism are using someone else's laboratory results and submitting them as one's own. Even when students work in the lab as a group, each should endeavour to get the results recorded in her or his own notebook in case he or she is the one assigned to carry out the experiment while someone else is assigned to write it down, or count it down as the case may be.

I had a funny experience with a classmate of mine in my final year. As usual, I volunteered to carry out most of the hands-on practical work and she willingly wrote down the results. As expected, we had to plot all the graphs from the experiment and write it up as an essay while in the lab, which I did. To my utmost surprise, asking this girl for the written-down results almost turned into a drama sketch, as she maintained that doing that was an act of plagiarism. "Plagiarism, my foot!" I retorted.

Her explanation was that I should have written the results down while carrying out the experiment simultaneously, and an attempt to copy them from her lab notebook amounted to plagiarism. I could hardly believe what I heard. Only on the intervention of fellow students and the laboratory assistant was I bailed out from that ridiculous scenario.

Boy, did I learn a good lesson from that! It was just an example of extremism when it comes to abiding with simple university rules and regulations. I met students who were just plain selfish who would use any silly explanation to excuse their unreasonable behaviour. Some would even decline to explain unclear areas during revision classes and term it in some funny manner. If I was really unclear about anything, they'd recommend that I speak to the lecturer in charge at a later time.

It seemed to me that students in the UK could be definitely selfish with their knowledge and understanding, contrary to what I knew back in Nigeria, where any student who excels in any subject is naturally expected to pass that knowledge on to others, mostly in the form of organising tutorials. That way, students can share knowledge and information on their best subjects while gaining from others in their strong subjects, but that is not really the norm in the UK, except in a few cases.

Knowing that it was often a case of an everyone-for-himself-and-God-for-everybody attitude with fellow students, I never hesitated in consulting the lecturers when I needed to do so. It didn't just help me build good relationships with the academic staff, but also gave me the opportunity to satisfy my inquisitive mind on an array of topics. Not that that was an everyday affair, but the few chances that I got were well worth it.

LEARNING GMT TIME KEEPING.

Please don't be alarmed when I talk about African time here. We Africans are well known for a laid-back attitude towards time-keeping. Frankly speaking, we just seem to flow with life with a cool rhythm, albeit to the detriment of some systems. I had been told about Brits' regimental time-keeping ethics but didn't quite expect it to be that religious. If a lecture is at 9.00 am, believe me, by 8.45am most students would be seated, and even the lecturer would be there some minutes before the start of the class.

That was a big leap for me, not that I was a customary latecomer by any chance, but strict time-keeping was relatively new to me. When in Rome, however, do as the Romans do, and in no time I thought that I was adjusting well to good time-keeping – until my newly developed manners were tested.

I had scheduled an appointment with a lecturer named Dr Brian to get a personal tutorial on some topics he had taught in class. He promised to spend an hour with me to clarify those areas, and it sounded like a good arrangement. The extra tutorial was to start at 10.00 am and was to last for approximately an hour, according to the plan.

On the set day, I walked into his office at about a quarter past the hour and realised that he was attending to someone else. He briefly excused himself and explained to me that the personal tutorial needed to be rescheduled since I didn't make it right on time. He said that my fifteen minutes of lateness had altered his whole plans.

For goodness' sake, I was only a mere fifteen minutes late! I tried persuading him to spend the remaining forty-five minutes, since I had missed the first fifteen, but he politely refused, saying that keeping to appointment times to the letter is as important as the appointment itself. I left the office with a long and confused face.

At the time, I couldn't just understand the fuss about mere fifteen minutes. It seemed to me that a mountain was just being made out of a molehill. I strutted away and narrated the incident to my cousin, who further explained how important it is to keep to time as far as British society is concerned.

Then it was a matter of adjusting to real Greenwich Mean Time and not using my own time estimates, at least as far as appointments were concerned. I can imagine the number of fellow African and other international students who have had similar experiences. Strict time-keeping would have been laughable issues to us, rather than this serious affair it was turning out to be.

In essence, understanding how the time-keeping culture works and adhering strictly to appointment times to save oneself from embarrassing situations is paramount for international students. It might not be our first culture, but I guess that is part of the education we have come to seek in a developed country.

DAY-TO-DAY CLASSROOM LIFE

Still settling into student life, it took quite a while to get used to the whole system, familiarising myself with the lecturers and fellow students. In no time, I had a few class buddies who went out of their way to help me and make me feel comfortable. Interestingly, some of the friendliest students were the deeply religious Muslim girls who wore the full veil and regalia.

One would have though that they wouldn't associate or socialise with others in the class, and, if they did, not with someone who dresses in a Westernised way like me. I thought that their faith would hinder free communication and friendliness between us. How wrong was I? They were extremely accommodating and welcoming. Even when I missed a few classes, they readily offered their help with lecture notes and material. If there was anything I saw about their faith manifesting in our relationships, it was the exuberant sense of generosity and kindness which they exuded.

Even when I questioned them about the rationale behind some of their beliefs, they were more than ready to explain as long as I didn't try to impress any other faith on them. No wonder my closest pals in class were Rabia, Feroza, and Faiza, who were deeply religious, yet enormously friendly.

On the other hand, there were a group of four girls who tried to make life miserable for a few of us. They weren't only terribly snobbish, but would hurl wraps of paper at others at random from where they sat at the back of the class. I realised that they saw this as a good game, and I became one of their main targets. In the bid to avoid any contact with them, I constantly changed where I sat in class and ensured that I didn't sit where they could hurl their paper balls. I mentioned it once to the other African girl in the class, who had lived in the UK for a few years. She said that it was nothing other than bullying.

Bullying? I wasn't used to such a word and certainly not at university. I wouldn't have described the situation as such, seeing it merely as students playing naughty pranks. Her explanation was that it could be an attempt to elicit an angry reaction from me, knowing that I'm a new student in the class and from Africa, too. She mentioned that there is a stereotype about Africans that we react aggressively, and that might be their way of provoking me. She further explained that a number of students would like to try my limits as a foreign student, just to know how far they could go with me and what they could get away with. If I put up with it, they'd try worse things, but if I expressed my disapproval at the onset they would surely back off because they are cowards and hate confrontations. At the time, her explanation made no meaning to me and it was just hard to comprehend.

True to her words, the next time they started their tantrums I summoned enough courage to turn around and ask the group who exactly had thrown the sweet wrap at me.

To my dismay, these girls, who had previously acted strong and confident, became uneasy and jittery. Each of them tried denying it, saying that it was the other, but I made it clear to them that I had only kept quiet over time, but that did not mean that I was unaware that they were the culprits. Immediately, they apologised as a group and said that it was going to be the end of their games. After that simple confrontation, those actions were never repeated. It was all part of the learning curve, after all.

As expected, there were different cliques and loyalty groups in the class, which meant that certain people had permanent designated seats. Not that it was a formal arrangement, but students had personalised spaces and seats. If, for example, a member of a clique wasn't in class yet, his or her seat would still be reserved and no other person would be allowed to sit there. Funny politics in the classroom, I'd call it.

Noise-making and loud chatting were other items that characterised the class. The lecturers would often have to plead for peace and quiet. That never ceased to remind me of my primary and secondary-school classes. Irrespective of how old or mature students are, they still act like school pupils. Just hearing the market place-like noises and chit-chat told me that students would always be students.

Something that was a bit strange to me at the time was a ten-minute break we had at the top of every hour in between lectures. Most lecture slots lasted for an hour anyway, but we had these short breaks before the next one started.

If that wasn't new enough to me, I realised that most people were munching on snacks. So, for the first few hours of the day in class, an individual might munch a pack of crisps, a bar of chocolate, and a piece of cake, and of course slurp down a cup of hot chocolate, tea, or coffee. I usually wondered why people had to eat almost every hour, and then they'd be off at noon for lunch break, come back to the class in the afternoon, and still keep munching.

Only heaven knows how much they spent on food and snacks a day. I mean, this was just outrageous. Didn't they ever stop eating? Snacking seemed to be an important tradition in studying in this country. No wonder I met many students pot-bellied from feasting on all the junk food the world offers.

∽

CHAPTER 9
COLOURED AND MIGHTY DISCOVERY: I AM BLACK!

In my mind and from what I had gathered, racism was a phased-out social phenomenon which occurred centuries ago. Little did I know that it still exists in British society. Even though I hardly experienced it in class or in any official setting at university, I was still faced with traces of it.

Prior to living in the UK, if you had asked me what the colour of my skin was, I would have said "brown," or "chocolate," but certainly not black. All of a sudden, I realised that people referred to me, whenever the occasion demanded, as being black. It seemed as if a light bulb had been momentarily switched on. So, after all, I am black. That was a great discovery for my very brown self. What I got to know was that as long as a person has Negroid genes, no matter how light in complexion she or he is, people would still refer to that person as being black.

One Nigerian student whom I knew to be so fair in complexion that it almost looked like she lacked the melanin in her skin found it difficult to believe that people were referring to her as being black. She told me that for once she felt black all her life. Of course, the black classification is based on a racial group identity rather than being an exact description of a person's skin fairness or colour.

My first encounter with racism was in the second-year class. We had been given a case study presentation to work on in a group. The lecturer in charge had assigned different members of the class into the groups in which we were expected to work. I was the only black student in my group. It wasn't an issue as far as I was concerned, but I realised that after various responsibilities had been assigned to each of us, the lady I had to work with, Sobbie, was avoiding me. I didn't understand what was going on, and so after classes on a particular day, I walked up to her to ask for us to work together in doing our part.

She snapped at me in front of some of our classmates and said that if I wanted to do the work I should do it alone and not ask her any questions. She walked away immediately, leaving me confused. I tried on many other occasions to speak to her, but she evaded me as much as she could.

The next step I took was speaking to the group leader, who pacified me and apologised on her behalf. He informed me that she had actually complained to him about working with me because she didn't want to work with a black person, her reason being that black people are generally rough and aggressive. Unknown to me at the time, the two words, 'rough' and 'aggressive' are commonly used in the larger society for stereotyping black people.

I was shocked and perplexed by such remarks since I had done nothing to her and she hardly knew me. The only encounters she'd had with me previously were in the general classroom, so I didn't understand her stereotype of me being a rough and aggressive person based on my colour. The team leader, who was of Pakistani origin, tried to calm me down and advised me to do my part of the work and to ignore her.

As far as I was concerned the issue needed to be resolved, since we still had the group coursework to hand in and time was no longer on our side. I wanted to get to the root of the matter since I didn't want to lose out on any of the marks.

A few days later we were having practical sessions in the laboratory. I walked up to her, knowing that she couldn't avoid me or walk away. On enquiring about her comments about me, she became extremely defensive, saying that she just didn't want to work with me and she was reserving the right not to explain her reason. I informed her that Ahmid, the team leader, had spilled the beans and that I knew what her reason was. In the course of our discussion, I threatened to make a report of her racist comments to the university authorities. I noticed that she was a bit apprehensive and tried denying the claim immediately.

Later that evening, Sobbie sent a friend of hers to talk me out of making a report, saying that she was sorry for making such a comment. Her friend went on saying that what Sobbie said shouldn't be taken seriously and that we still needed to work cordially together in the future as classmates.

What I noticed after this incident was that Sobbie began acting extremely paranoid around me. Since I didn't report her, she thought I would be out to get her via another means someday. She would often ask me if she had done anything wrong to me whenever we were made to work together or whether I had any problems with her. I reckon she understood the weight of her words and the possible consequences.

Even though I had threatened to make a report, I didn't think that reporting her would have been the solution to the problem. What was more, she was of an ethnic minority background herself, being of Pakistani origin. If I was expecting anyone to be directly racist towards me, I would have imagined that it would have been a Caucasian, certainly not a Pakistani girl. That was the most ridiculous thing that I could imagine. That someone whose family is from a developing country like mine could brand me in such a manner was overwhelming.

Many laws are in place to reduce the incidents of racist abuse and attacks, but what I have come to realise is that they are not the most effective weapons. Racist attacks and incidents still take place every day, and to an extent as a black person I have had to live with them. The government tries to clamp down on racism, but I know that it would take more than the law to eradicate it. It's something that parents bring their children up with, so that when they grow up it becomes their way of life by default.

How do you explain a four-year-old girl who says that her mum had instructed her not to relate to black people because they don't take baths, which is the reason for their darkened skin colour? How do you combat the social discrimination you observe even in public places when someone speaks to a Caucasian with utmost respect and tenderness, then turns to a black person within the same context with a rude and nonchalant attitude when there is no difference between them but skin colour? The only thing about racism here is that it is subtle and often dressed up with excuses.

Although my first experience of racism was at university, it was extremely rare there. With most students it is not obvious as long as we live on campus with little or no contact with the outside world.

We hardly experience prejudice as long as we stay within the university premises. Stepping out of the boundaries of the university, especially if we take up a part-time job, would be the first place to inform us that our skin colour makes us different and that we might be treated differently from the majority.

Interestingly, British-born blacks understand better the dynamics of racial prejudice than an immigrant like me. I narrated my ordeal in class to a Black British friend, expressing with shock that I didn't believe that certain people could be so narrow-minded to think that having melanin in your skin defines your personality and intelligence level. She just laughed at my remarks and welcomed me into the real world.

She told me that if I believed that prejudice was non-existent in British society I was living in a fool's paradise. If I was indeed living in a fool's paradise, I sure had a number of neighbours on the street who thought exactly like me. Apparently, as far as she was concerned the world of absolute equality that I had in mind was only a mirage and not to be expected in the real world.

I could then understand why the society appears to be segregated. In most cases, Asians live in one end of the city, blacks live in their own areas, while the whites have their own world. It wouldn't take long living in the system to observe this. On most of the jobs I took, I observed that colour segregation patterns were mostly present. Of course, there are a few exceptions to the rule, because younger people are much more open-minded, but it doesn't erase the reality that racial divides still exist in the society.

If I was shocked by the classroom experience, a ruder shock was in store for me with my next experience of prejudice. It was in a church in the Bradford area. I had been invited to a youth programme, which I gladly attended. The vicar of the church seemed friendly at first and made enquiries about me and my country of origin, to which I gave answers. He told me that the church had a youth volunteer worker from another African country.

As though he didn't realise that I was an African as well, he blurted out about how all these wretched Africans come into the UK to live on "their" resources, that the volunteer was from an impoverished background and they were trying to offer some assistance, and that a number of Africans only come into the UK to attend school and to get social welfare benefits. His opinion was that they are mainly dependant on the government for sustenance.

As he went on about the poor and irresponsible Africans, I reminded him that I was an African, too, and that not all of us migrate into the UK to live on the system. I further explained that as an international student, I pay a fortune for my education annually. I was seriously indignant about his remarks and his stereotype of Africans. It sounded as if to him Africans are a bunch from a country rather than a continent, and are nothing but social-security cases in the UK.

Africa is such an enormous continent, and it has many different cultures and peoples. For example, those from North Africa have a totally different way of life to us in West Africa or those in Southern Africa. The vicar's generalisation about Africa and Africans showed that he didn't seem to understand Africa's variety. What people like him don't realise is that although they classify all Africans as paupers, we are made to pay as much as nine times the home-students' fees and bring many resources into the educational system. That concept on its own beggars a lot of questions.

When I told him of my status as an international student and not a state welfare case, he further probed by asking if my parents were top government officials in my country. Even though he didn't explain the rationale behind his question, I suspected that he asked it because he might have presumed that only top government officials in Africa who embezzle funds could afford to sponsor their wards to UK universities. That was a question a number of people had asked me before.

With a sense of irritation, I replied that not only government officials had enough to send their children abroad. In actual fact, neither of my parents was employed by the government at the time, and many people from my country as well as other African countries sponsor their children abroad for educational purposes without necessarily embezzling funds.

What people like the vicar do not understand is that all the international students from Africa being funded by their immediate families aren't the pauperised Africans that they know. For an average African family to afford thousands of pounds annually for tuition fees, that family would be from at least the upper-middle or higher class of society. Unfortunately, all Africans are presumed to live from hand to mouth.

The most ridiculous part of my time with the vicar was that he told me of his charity work in Kenya and how they wanted to help the people of Africa. How paradoxical could it be that he stereotyped and resented Africans, didn't think so well of them, yet was offering acts of charity which ought to be hallmarked by love.

Maybe his opinion of Africans is that of people who deserve no humane respect, but live on the doles handed out by charitable organisations. I felt like telling him to stop his charity work in Kenya and be kind and nice to the Africans he met on a regular basis in his country. His charity could at least begin at home. I left in an upset mood, vowing never to visit the church again. If I had not met other Christians in the UK, I would have been misinformed into thinking that most of them hold the same impression about us Africans. It is religious people like him who give Christianity a bad image in the world.

Could I really blame him, though, when some of our corrupt African leaders see charity dole-outs as the solution to the quagmire the continent seemingly lies in? When we Africans become as enterprising as the Chinese and Japanese people, who utilise their countries' potential and export finished products to the rest of the world, maybe we'd get the dignity and respect we have deserved for so long. For once, I was seeing Africa and her populace with the eyes of an outsider. The Africa I was proud of was being downtrodden before my very eyes and I was forced to partake in her shame.

It's even more interesting that even Black British people would try to dissociate themselves from Africa like a plague. I'd hear some of them speak of Africa in a derogatory manner, as though it is a cursed continent with no inch of worth to the world.

If it's not the Africa that is always dying or warring that the media portrays, it is usually the sickly or poverty-stricken Africa. It is hardly ever the Africa that has great potential. A continent with nations that have moved rapidly from colonial rule into independence in a few decades, or that has produced such world-renown figures as Nelson Mandela, Kofi Annan, Emeka Anyaoku, Fela Anikulapo-Kuti, and Professor Wole Soyinka, the English-language Nobel laureate novelist. If I had not been born and bred in an African country, the portrayal of Africa in the Western media would have convinced me that the continent is nothing but a dead man's land.

Seeing the great Africa I knew and cherished in tatters from another perspective was indeed humbling. I could see that even though giant strides have been made in Africa, much more needs to be done in order to further development and progress.

As I mentioned, racial discrimination still persists in the UK, but it is dressed up in different, more-appealing costumes. I was surprised when I went into a major bookstore in London and discovered that a section of the store was labelled "black writing". To clarify what this meant, I decided to look objectively at the headline with a wide perspective. Maybe that section had books specifically on black people's issues or our world.

To my dismay, the section was reserved for black authors irrespective of the title of the book. The books didn't necessarily address issues in the black world because some of them had universal topics and messages to the world. Of course, I wasn't going to let the matter rest. I requested to speak to the store manager, just to know the purpose for segregating black authors into a section. She attended to me, and after I asked her she didn't have any explanation, either, only that it was the company's policy. There might be valid reasons for that segregation, but it would be interesting to know the rationale behind calling a section "black writing" in such a large bookstore.

How appropriate would it be to label a section of the bookshop "white" or "Asian writing"? Is there something unique about a black person writing? Is it mutually exclusive to be black and to be a writer? I am still asking questions until I get appropriate answers.

BROWN, BLACK, WHITE, GREEN, PINK GREY OR ORANGE?

Racial prejudice and stereotypes cut across the boundaries and settings of colour. If it's not an Englishman who considers a Caucasian Irish fellow to be stupid, it's often the banter between the Afro-Caribbean person and a black African, or a prejudice against Eastern Europeans.

The racial clash between Jamaicans and Nigerians in London is something that I have never been able to understand. Knowing full well that, historically, a high percentage of people from the Caribbean island of Jamaica have their roots in Nigeria, the rivalry between them might only be the clash of the titans. Prejudice is nothing but a parochial approach to life and people.

If there was anything I formerly believed, I thought that racial prejudice is only based on colour, but I was proven wrong. Prejudice is just an irrational bias with which narrow-minded people view any other person who appears different to them. A person don't need to act wrong; all that people need to do is be who they are for them to be offensive to a racist. Their mere existence is what triggers the reactions, not necessarily what they have done or not done.

Once I was at work, and the lady I worked with told me that an English expression for stupid would be to say that someone is Irish. I totally believed her, but didn't understand where the saying originated from. In addition to teaching me the new English slogan, she warned me not to use it when any Irish colleague was around. I then knew that it was a way of denigrating an Irish person and not a basic English slogan, after all. Now, an Irishman, who is white, still faces discrimination from some English folks in the same way as a black or an Asian person.

As history has it, it was the Irish and black people who were the main objects of racial discrimination in England back in the sixties. A sign in public places, "No Irish, No Blacks, and No Dogs Allowed," said it all. The subtle discrimination still holds. Something that I have observed is that Irish people or their descendants in England are more friendly and welcoming to an average black person or immigrant. Knowing the history of how both groups were ostracised in society, it could be that the average Irish person identifies with the discrimination to which black people have often been subjected.

If it's not the Scottish against the English, it is the English against the Welsh, or the Cornish people, who claim to be anti-English. It seems like prejudice is a trait people use to justify their xenophobic and homophobic feelings. I thought that the tribal clashes in Africa were only limited to us, not knowing that they exist in the UK, too, although covertly subtle in nature. The root causes are often irrational and illogical. There might be cultural differences between people of different backgrounds, but I doubt if they justify any hatred whatsoever towards them.

It seems like the less educated and exposed people are the more prejudiced they are, but intellectual ability doesn't necessarily stand as the yardstick for measuring racial prejudice. I've heard of a professor who proposed the theory that black people are less intellectually capable than whites. As highly educated and well travelled as he is, he still postulates such erroneous ideas, so it shows that education might only disguise the prejudice better in an intellectual than in an uneducated person.

The interesting thing about racism and prejudice is that some white people would go to any extent to fight the societal evil which some of their own folks seek to uphold. Of course, such anti-racist whites are usually subjected to ridicule and attacks as well, be it socially or professionally. Some of the people who stand up staunchly against racism are whites who have known the damaging effects in their communities. I always admire such people and often praise them for their bold and undaunted stands. Someone can choose to stand up against parochial minds is worthy of honour.

༄

CHAPTER 10
HEALTH ISSUES: HEALTH-CENTRE REGISTRATION

On arrival at the university, one of the first places I had to register, other than the student registry and the bank, was with a general practitioner, commonly referred to as a GP, at the university health centre. The GP is the main point of call for an individual's health needs. Without being registered with a GP, it would be difficult to get treated in a hospital except in an emergency.

We were notified of GP surgeries close by, but the one assigned to all students was based at the university health centre. At the time I didn't understand how important it was to register with a doctor, since the system didn't work like that in Nigeria. More interestingly, nobody is expected to pay for the registration, doctor's consultation, and treatment, except for the medications prescribed.

After a few weeks at the university, I eventually got registered at the university health centre and had a GP assigned to me. For health checks and any medical records required, students normally contact their GP. Every individual's health-management issues are the GP's responsibility.

I didn't fully understand how the medical and health system in the UK worked, but became familiarised with it in time. Medical treatment is basically free to all residents, and the health system is based on the National Health Service (NHS), which has primary-care trusts, mental-health trusts, counselling units, hospitals, and clinics operating under it.

Irrespective of people's status and social background, they are entitled to free health care in the UK. The NHS is one of the best facilities, if not the best, in the UK, where people can have even specialist treatments like plastic surgery and in-vitro fertilisation absolutely free, but with the taxpayers ultimately funding everything. Even though some people regularly abuse the NHS's services, it boasts being one of the best health systems in the world. A system in which free healthcare is accessible to all and sundry is a great feat for any country that considers its citizenry to be worthwhile enough for life.

I now understand how people enjoy longevity in spite of their social status in the UK. It is indeed sad that such basic needs of life as access to the simplest healthcare facilities is denied millions in the world today. If my stay in the UK has imprinted anything firmly on my heart, it is to value health and to view access to it as a necessity for life and not a luxury for some. As much as some of us believe in life after death, it is impressive to see people believing in life before death, too.

In addition to the basic health requirements the NHS provides, there are other programmes which I would have thought should be paid for by their users. Some of these are a smoking-quitting programme and schemes for drug addicts who are facing withdrawal symptoms. Those help and support services are luxuries if one considers the poor health infrastructure in Nigeria, for example.

Even more impressive is that many patients receive all their drug prescriptions for free, depending on the ailments they suffer from.

Patients who live with conditions that need to be tightly monitored, such as diabetes and coronary heart disease, have their medical bills picked up by their local health authorities. Depending on people's family income, health condition, and age, they could be entitled to free prescriptions.

My GP was a middle-aged woman who swapped shifts with another middle-aged doctor from time to time. I often wondered what their working lives were like if most of their consultations with patients were anything like the ones they had with me. Boring would be the ideal word to describe what I observed.

Whenever I complained of any ailment or issue, they usually asked me to open my mouth, flashed their pen torch down my throat, checked my pulse with their stethoscopes, and asked myriad questions. I wouldn't have been too concerned with them, except they seemed to prescribe only paracetamol and ibuprofen for every ailment under the sun. Be it a cold, sore throat, runny nose, skin irritation, or swollen gland, they would always write one of those two prescriptions, and it is impossible to buy drugs over the counter in a pharmacy without a doctor's prescription, which made some of the instances frustrating.

For example, I had a persistent cold which resulted in coughing, sneezing, and other symptoms, for which they prescribed me paracetamol tablets. I knew that there was more to the cold than a mere change of climates and weather, but my GP insisted that I take paracetamol or ibuprofen. I continually complained to him about the symptoms, but he wouldn't change his mind. I read a number of books and journal articles on the symptoms I had in order to have an idea of what was wrong with me.

From those, I learnt that I needed more than the doctor's prescriptions for analgesics. I went back and suggested that I be prescribed a nasal spray. In the end, the new GP I was assigned to gave in to my request. The nasal spray worked amazing wonders, and that was the end of an ailment that had once been associated with my change of environment from the tropics to the cold.

My experiences taught me that even though GPs are specially trained in their field, it might be worthwhile to read extensively on my ailments or symptoms if I didn't feel that my health issues were being addressed adequately. That could even help the GP in making a better diagnosis and treatment.

There was the case of a man who constantly complained of stomach pains to his GP, who dismissed the complaints as nothing but a case of an ulceric stomach. The patient kept complaining to the GP, who ordered no medical tests. The complaints continued incessantly, and GP was forced to send his blood specimen for some diagnostic tests. Unfortunately, the young fellow had a malignant form of stomach cancer which was widespread at the time of diagnosis. Even though he was given some treatments to combat the damage done, he lost the fight to cancer within six months and died. That is an extreme case of medical neglect which isn't an everyday occurrence, but it is still worthwhile to insist on getting the necessary check-ups and diagnostic tests if symptoms persist, especially as an international student with no family members around.

With the health service in the UK, people can call for the GP to see them at home if they feel too weak to move out, or call for ambulance service simply by dialling 999. For someone like me who wasn't used to this kind of rapid-response service, it was hugely impressive.

On weekends and other times when people feel ill, they should contact the accident and emergency unit, or A&E, at the nearest hospital. The impression I had from the name A&E was that it was reserved for accident victims and those who had life-threatening conditions. How wrong was I?

The A&E unit in all the hospitals attend to anyone who feels that their ailment needs urgent attention if their GP is inaccessible at the time. Of course, the GP should be the first port of call, but no one should hesitate to walk into the A&E if their health seems to be failing or getting out of hand.

∽

CHAPTER 11

AM I COMMUNICATING OR MERELY SPEAKING?

Back in Nigeria, I was educated right from reception class to university in the English language, and every student had to take an A-level standard English test as part of the exams needed for matriculation into any Nigerian university. Even at university, the use of English was a compulsory course in the first year. Based on this thorough training in English, I felt confident about studying in the UK. Little did I know that I would still need to learn another style of English on arrival. Maybe all I succeeded in doing was merely speak and did not communicate, after all.

In formal terms things seemed okay, since I could read and write fluently in English, but when it got to verbal expressions, I discovered that it was almost a matter of unlearning what I knew and learning a whole new idiom. For one thing, people use many colloquialisms when speaking, so that people who are unaccustomed to slang and sayings can basically get lost in the midst of conversations.

Let me start with the expression, 'in it,' which sounds more like *inni*, and actually means 'isn't it.' How on earth can 'isn't it' be transcribed as 'inni' in verbal form? Of course, Yorkshire people seem to have their own coined words, which are amazingly different to the Queen's English, which we are taught back in Africa. They refer to money as 'brass' and say 'ta' instead of 'thank you'. At first, I didn't understand why people would say 'ta' as a way of expressing appreciation.

The intensity with which we were taught English in Nigeria was such that an average Nigerian who has passed through the formal educational system can communicate to a notably high standard in the English language. We weren't just taught the grammatical use of English, but the language's vocabulary and semantics.

All of a sudden, all those language skills with which I thought I was so well equipped were being rigorously tested and sometimes battered. I guess people considered some of the English I spoke to be outdated. I said to someone that a lady had "put to bed," and I was queried as to what that meant. When I explained that it was an idiomatic expression for "giving birth to a baby," I was seriously laughed at. Maybe it was better to keep my idioms to myself and fellow Nigerians after all.

What about people asking me repeatedly if I understood English or what they are saying? No matter how well I communicated, at times I realised that my ability in verbal communication was still questioned. People assumed that I wouldn't understand certain words, for example and made efforts to explain them while all eyes were in my direction, implying that I needed assistance. These were just part of the day-day dealings I faced.

Inspite of saying that English is the official language of my country and that I could understand quite clearly what was being said, it still occurred regularly. I discovered that a number of other international students were faced with this predicament, and quite frankly it could be a bit embarrassing at times. Still, I tried to see the funny side of it most of the time.

I had my African accent, all right, but I can say that my command of English grammar was much better than many of those people's. The kind of grammar I was hearing was too strange to believe. I'd hear statements like, "I was talking to you yesterday, wasn't I?" or "We was eating there, inni?" It was almost like the only question tag used was inni, even when it didn't correlate with the question asked.

Another interesting trait about Brits is that they rarely speak their minds directly. I always have to read in between the lines to grasp fully what they say. If I asked for a favour, for example, instead of saying either a "Yes" or a "No," the common responses are, "I'll see what I can do," or "Maybe." They might respond that they'll try their best, but more often than not, they avoid outright, direct responses.

At first I thought they were joking with these statements, but later got to know that that's the way some people speak. How on earth did these people pass their GCSE English or A-level Standard English, which we are mandated to pass before gaining admission into any Nigerian university? In my opinion, some of the natives need those English tests as much as the foreigners. If we take English as a second or third language, the original speakers should be perfectly fluent too, I thought.

Funnily enough, however, another group of individuals seemed to be fascinated by my command of English. Others asked me whether I came over to UK to learn English. It wasn't unusual to be asked how I was able to speak and comprehend the language so well. Some of my Nigerian friends and I would often discuss these funny trends and take those comments lightly.

On quite a few occasions I have heard people ask some of us to speak posh, meaning to pronounce words singly and clearly, as opposed to the northern English accents in which people mumble up their words, not saying each word without adjoining it to the next. Honestly, I just laughed over those comments. I try to speak as clearly as I can, but posh I know nothing about.

On the other hand, there are those who would tell me that I don't speak right and that they can't understand a word I'm saying. More often than not, they hardly even take the pain to listen to me. As long as a person's accent isn't native, it comes across as though all they do is just switch off and moan about that person not speaking right. All anyone needs to do to catch them out is to say something rude and from the blue; the same person who couldn't understand suddenly knows and grasps exactly what has been said.

I noticed that a number of Chinese students usually employed this trick. If they didn't want to talk to me, they'd immediately feign ignorance of understanding English, but if a person says something offensive within the same premises they'd give that a swift response.

YORKSHIRE AND NORTHERN ENGLISH

Yorkshire people, referred to as Tykes, have their own ways of life and communication. They are known for their sense of humour, straight-talking and down-to-earth frankness.

In the north of England, and particularly in Yorkshire where I studied and lived, it sounds as if they speak a slightly different language to that which is spoken in the southern part of the country and in London. Besides their accents being varied and different, certain expressions and words mean different things. Of course, there is the southern and northern divide that results in the banter between the so-called posh southerners and their northern counterparts.

In Yorkshire, for example, it sounds like people usually elongate the pronunciation of their words with a special emphasis on the vowels. It sounded rhythmical and funny to me at the time and it took me a long time to understand fully what people said. I thought it was only the local languages we speak in Nigeria and other African countries that get such varied dialects, but, alas, the same applies in the UK.

Words like mum, love, and come would be pronounced as though the vowel is the "o", in "oat" or "old", so when a Tyke says love, it sounds like *loave*. Also, the endearment generally used in addressing people is 'love', rather than the 'darling' commonly used down South. I just needed to be in a shop or on the streets before I heard someone say, "All right, love," or "Are you okay, love?" What was more, I wasn't used to these darling-love-sweetie endearments where I came from. We only use endearments in addressing the special people in our lives, not any Tom, Dick, or Harry on the street.

Salutations down South are usually "hello" or "hi," but up North people greet each other with "hiya". Even more interesting about dialects, accents, and variants of spoken English in the North, as it is in other parts, is that the way people speak still differs from town to town or city to city, and most of the accents have different names, too.

My first experience with Scouse, the accent spoken in Liverpool, another city in the north of England, was when a Scouser Liverpudlian classmate of mine gave a presentation to the whole class. The rising and falling tone and pitches of her words were both funny and captivating to me. To be honest, it sounded a bit like speaking English with my Yoruba accent, and it sounded a bit like Scottish English too. That actually made it more interesting.

The natives of Manchester, who are called Mancunians, speak a bit differently from Liverpudlians and Tykes, even though each city is only about an hour's drive from Manchester. Further North again are the Geordies, who are the people from Tyneside-Newcastle area. These have a wide vocabulary different from the whole of England, and the dialect different, too. Getting to grasp these dialects and accents was a tug of war at first, but with careful listening, I became well versed with them.

My informal education with these expressions and dialects had only just started. One of my classmates was away from classes for a few days, so I decided to ask her on her return if she was okay. She told me that she had been "poorly" and had been on medications. That she was on medications told me she must have been ill, but what was that word she used? "Poorly"? I'd never heard that before, but it means "unwell" or "sick". Being sick commonly refers to vomiting rather than being unwell. I was just wondering where they were conjuring all these words from and how I had spoken in English all my life and never heard them.

One of the funniest expressions I heard in Yorkshire was "you float my boat", said with a deep Yorkshire accent. I reeled in unquenchable laughter when I learnt what it means. In the usual Yorkshire manner, "my" is pronounced as "mai". Imagine a guy saying those words, stretching the vowels, to a lady as a means of expressing an interest in her, or that he fancies her. That expression on its own was just too funny to me, and of course the accent didn't make it any better.

A particular Yorkshireman that I worked with, Bob, was a lively and friendly man, but spoke with such a strong accent that all I could do was smile and say thank-you at whatever he said, not minding what it was. Even when the response to what he said didn't warrant a thank-you or smile, I did, because I didn't want to ask him to repeat everything he said. He caught me out once and asked why I smiled and thanked him irrespective of what he said.

My explanation was straightforward and honest: that I didn't clearly comprehend what he said most of the time and didn't want to bother him, since I knew he didn't have an awful attitude and wasn't saying horrible things, either. After that episode, he took time to speak a bit more slowly when talking to me and never hesitated to ask each time if I understood what he said – nice, helpless man!

Words such as a "tenner" for a ten-pound note, a "fiver" for five pounds, and a "cuppa" for a cup of tea were other typical idioms I learnt in time.

MENTION THE MAGIC WORDS

These aren't words from the fairy godmother or the world of talismans, but are used for getting by and around. A failure to use them may infer that a person is rude, demanding, and uncivilised. English's two magic words are 'please' and 'thank you'. I discovered that any request made has to be made with a please, even if an older or senior person is speaking to a junior or subordinate.

For someone like me who wasn't brought up with this compulsive pleading for anything or everything with the use of the word please, it was plainly odd. Why on earth I had to ask for every damn thing by saying please when I wasn't necessarily requesting a favour was beyond me. If I wanted to buy a train ticket, for example, I had to say, "Can I buy a ticket, please?" Even for buying a cup of tea it has to be, "A cup of tea, please."

Any attempt not to use this word is considered to be extremely rude and commanding. Note that I said extremely, because the person at the other end sees the speaker as making a demand rather than a request, which he or she has the right to decline since it hasn't been politely presented.

In the same vein, if someone asks a question to check if someone else wants something or not, the magic words must still come into play in the reply. A positive response has to be, "Yes, please," and a negative one, "No, thanks." An answer such as a plain Yes or No is considered impolite. No wonder the British are said to be the most polite people on the planet. Maybe too polite for keeps in this regard.

Interestingly, in response to these questions about whether someone wants something or not, "please" implies a "yes", while "thanks" or "thank you" simply means "no". How on earth could I have figured these things out, for crying out loud? No English textbook teaches these, or maybe I have just been unfortunate not to come across one yet.

Getting a grasp of these simple communication techniques makes living in the UK a lot easier. I'm sure you'd agree with me that things like these are alien to an average African, and that not using them as often as the Brits do isn't a show of rudeness at all, but simply a difference in communication patterns.

Still talking about the magic words, there are other magic patterns of speaking that I came to know, with the use of 'would' and 'could'. Either of these two words indicate whether you are ordering someone to do something or making a request. Being foreign to some of these patterns, I asked a boss of mine at work if she would get me some materials on the top shelf in the laboratory. I was on a student-placement programme in the company at the time, which was after I had been in the UK a year. It shows how long it can take really to understand a lot of the ways people communicate and the real implications of what they are saying.

On that fateful day, I said, "Please Rosie, would you like to get me those chemicals on the top cupboard?"

The other member of staff present said, "Oh! She is so commanding that she wouldn't even give you a choice in the matter."

I stood there bewildered at those comments, as Rosie corroborated what the other lady said. Seeing that I was a bit confused, they were kind enough to explain to me that using the phrase "would you" meant I was asking the person to carry out an action categorically; telling him or her what I wanted done but saying "could you" meant that I was making a request which the hearer could grant at her or his discretion. I was taking fresh lessons on the use of English there and then.

One African lady I once worked with almost got into trouble with some senior members of staff just because of this "would you" and "could you" issue. Any time she was asked, "Would you like to clean this?" or "Would you like to do that?" she'd respond by saying, "No." She wasn't interested in carrying out the tasks, and in her opinion she had a choice. What she didn't realise was that a question wasn't being posed to her, but rather she was being instructed what to do in the polite British manner.

When she was reported to the manager, she innocently stated her case that she was asked to register her interest in certain matters and she politely turned them down. At the time, she had only lived in the UK for a few months, which explained her actions, but what about someone like me who only figured that out after a year?

How funny is it that the same things said to different people can be taken in totally different ways. I discovered that some of the things I frowned at when spoken to were just the normal way people communicate over here in the UK, and some of the things I said casually were taken either too seriously or out of context, portraying me in a different light.

A friend of mine and I were having a dialogue, when all of a sudden she said, "Don't be silly, that's not the right thing to do."

What? Referring to me as an outright silly person? I didn't hesitate to register my displeasure for being called a silly person, but she maintained that she had not done so. All she meant by that was to advise me not to act or talk in a way that could be construed as being silly.

Where I am from, that isn't considered to be a piece of advice or warning, but a direct insult. Over time, I realised that telling someone not to be silly is synonymous to asking them to act correctly or to get straightened up, in a friendly context, of course. In the same way, when someone asks if another is mad, it doesn't mean that their sanity is being questioned, but if they are upset or angry.

One case of this involved an aunty's daughter. She was left in the care of my sister and she started putting up some naughty acts. My sister frowned at her and told her to sit still or else she would be in trouble. The young girl asked, "Aunty, are you mad?" My sister repeated the question to her and corrected her that she shouldn't say such rude things to older people.

The girl insisted that my sister was obviously mad. She said, "Aunty, I can see that you are really mad. I'll be a good girl from now on."

We were shocked to the bone that a little girl of her age could ask that question, which to us meant, "Are you insane or mentally disturbed?" In reality, the word mad in that context doesn't mean being a nutter.

POLITICALLY CORRECT SPEECH

As part of speaking acceptably in society, I learnt that I needed to be politically correct (commonly known as PC) so that my words offended nobody. PC language uses words and ideas that do not offend anyone based on their race, gender, culture, age, or disability. For someone like me who was from a different continent, the issues posed as political correctness did not make too much sense at the outset.

I was made aware that words like 'half-caste' used in referring to people of mixed ethnic backgrounds was politically incorrect. The correct word to use would be to refer to the person as a 'mixed-race' person. Mixed race was completely out of my imagination, since I know that there is only one race, after all: the human race. Mixed race sounded to me like someone with both human and non-human parents, but since that was the accepted, politically correct word, I learnt to adjust.

Some other PC words would be to recognise both genders when addressing authority figures. Instead of using 'Sir' in a letter, the PC way would be to use 'Sir/Ma' so as to avoid any offence. A whole array of words and ideas are considered to be politically incorrect and would be extremely rude to use, such as saying Paki in referring to a Pakistani person or Nigger or Negro in referring to someone of Afro-Caribbean descent. I doubt if I have quite grasped the whole expanse of this political correctness, but I am learning every day all the same.

To be PC is not to voice any concerns about some social issues because certain members of the larger society could be offended, and not to use certain words. To integrate fully into the UK system, understanding and speaking in politically correct terms is useful.

Part of PC speaking is to refer to those I would otherwise refer to as 'lazy' or not taking up employment in the society as being 'work shy'. Political correctness is all about making people feel dignified no matter what their status is. I found it a bit amusing and crazy at times, to be honest. That includes not speaking about such social issues as homosexuality or transsexuality in a derogatory manner, even though they appeared different to what I knew to be normal. At the end of the day, what is the standard yardstick for measuring normality when normal behaviour becomes relative in society? Learning political correctness further reminded me that I was living in a totally different world.

DEEP DOWN IN TROUBLE

If you want to get into trouble like I did when I first arrived in the UK, there are some innocent comments you'd need to make to people. I discovered that people are highly sensitive about their age and size. Someone like me, who didn't realise how serious these issues were, just commented on what I saw to be true.

Remember Becky, the girl who helped me with some notes on resumption into university? She was bigger than I was in stature and she looked somewhat older, as well. As we got talking, she told me her age and I passed a comment that she looked a lot older than her real age, and even more than me, although I was a few years older. Her change of countenance was immediate and disturbing. I didn't know that I had said something offensive at all. After all, I was only expressing myself.

I later got to know that people don't like to be described by their ages and any attempt to remind someone of his or her age could land me in a lot of trouble. I just needed to tell people that they look young, or younger than their age, and I'd make friends right away.

Back in Africa, where age is respected, people normally want to give the impression that they are older than their real ages, and I know of people who celebrated certain birthdays when they had not actually clocked those ages. The reverse is the case in the UK, and in the Western world in general. Almost everyone wants to be young and wants to believe so. How funny! Could it be a means of living in denial of the obvious? I leave that to your imagination.

Commenting on size, I almost got into trouble with my cousin's wife, who happens to be English. I saw her parents' photo portrait and said, "Oh! your dad is the slim one while your mum is fat."

You should have seen the shocked expression on her face. Her mouth was wide open in disbelief that I had passed such a rude comment. I just couldn't understand the wild reaction to what I thought was obvious. She reported to her husband, who took it up with me. He said, "You said my mother-in-law is fat, right?"

I replied, "Yes, I did. Can't you see that she's fat? Yeah, she's a fat person." I was wondering why a big fuss was made about my honest and complimentary comment. In Africa, a fleshy and robust woman is a sign of well-being and affluence. It is actually complimentary to tell a lady that she had put on some weight, and she'd be pleased to hear that. Not in the UK. Affluent and well-trimmed women are the slim-figured ones. Those who want to get others into a horrible mood just have to tell them how thay've put on some weight, and trouble will find them out wherever they are. How contradictory can cultures be?

Describing someone as being fat is considered to be one of the worst insults ever that a person could be sued for. Of course, I got a lecture that day from my cousin on how insulting my comment was and why I should never describe anyone as being fat. It was only because his wife understood that I didn't know the weight of my offence that I got away scot-free. How was I supposed to know that, anyway? I reckon that not using the word fat may be a way for obese people to live in denial of their state.

"Now that I have been barred from referring to people as being fat, how am I expected to describe them?" I asked. The polite versions, I was told, would be words like big or chubby. After living in the UK for a few years, I find it difficult to believe that I used some of those expressions with so much confidence and poise. I have shared the story with my friends many times and they end up laughing hysterically, also finding my former ill manners to be unbelievable.

Anyway, I have learnt my lessons and try not to comment on people's sizes and ages. I now know that I could refer to someone as being crazy and be more likely to get away with it than if I called that person an old man or woman or described her or him as being fat.

If you think those were bad, you need to hear of this next incident. I was in church one day with some group leaders and members of the choir when we got into a conversation. As the discussion progressed, I said that I was "pissed off" by what someone did. I was only trying to express my irritation at the act and nothing more, you see.

I just heard this sudden scream and yell from them. The leader I was with said, "Olanike, I can't believe you use such language, you know."

I was wondering what the language was, and to confirm my query repeated the statement, asking if that was what she meant. By now, they were totally displeased with me, but I still didn't understand what they were going on about. I'm sure by then they realised that I was oblivious to what the offence was. They kindly corrected me and explained the weight of the phrase I used. Imagine, I was using a vulgar swear word, and worse still, in church – and I was oblivious to it.

When I remember some of these incidents, I burst into uncontrollable laughter at myself, and I am trying to control that laughter now as I write. It wasn't that I was plain rude, but I was naïve and didn't understand what certain words meant in different societies and cultures.

I know a lot of my folks in Nigeria who use words such as piss and shit without thinking twice about what they mean, having heard too many of them spoken in Hollywood movies. Adding a bull in front of that shit word is even worse. We just didn't know that they were extremely vulgar and rude. Now, I find it difficult to utter those words, as I know how dirty and vulgar they sound, much more, contextually. I just picture those days of ignorance and get amused all by myself.

SAYINGS AND SLANG

There are other styles of communication that I only got used to with time. Sometimes I could figure out vaguely what the speaker was talking about, but the real interpretations of these sayings were nowhere in sight. Some of these colloquial terms and sayings include:

He's as good as a chocolate teapot, or a chocolate fire-guard, which means the person or thing referred to is useless.

To get a cob on, which means having a bad attitude or being in an awful mood, as in, "If Jack sees what you're doing, he's going to get a cob on."

You're going to comer cropper, which means you're going to get into trouble, as in, "She's comer cropper with the landlady for not paying the bills on time."

More work than a sick note, which means useless or of no value.

In fairness, most of these sayings are mostly spoken by people from the North of England. Londoners have their own cut-out vocabulary as well. People from the East End of London are called Cockneys, and their variant of English is referred to as Cockney English. They have their cockney rhyming slang, which I'd never figure out unless someone told me what each means. *Ruby Murray,* for instance, means curry, as in the food. *Apples and pears* means stairs, *kettle* means a wristwatch, and *a la mode* means a code, such as when people are speaking in a code that others are not meant to understand, such as in, "We had to talk a la mode at the bus stop." "We went up the apples and pears to say hello," means we went up the stairs. How on earth do people correlate these words with their intended meanings? It just sounds like a totally different language to me.

In need of some more cockney rhyming slang? *Anneka Rice* means advice, so if you're in need of Anneka Rice, I'm sure you now know where to go. *Ace of spades* means AIDS, the killer disease.

Please don't ask me how all these slang expressions came about because I'm clueless about their origins. How on earth do I explain that someone being dealt the ace of spades means he's got AIDS, or that *trouble and strife* means a wife? I'm sure a number of guys might say that they fully understand the root of that last expression, which could be considered offensive.

OTHER LANGUAGES IN THE UK?

If you are like me, you might have been tempted to believe that English is the island's only language, but after a few years I discovered that although English is the most popular and main language, some other languages are regionally recognised as official languages. Remember, the UK is made up of the four countries of England, Scotland, Wales, and Northern Ireland, but Great Britain comprises only the first three. I should have thought that other languages would be spoken by the nationals from the other countries, shouldn't I? Even these other nationals' English accents are sharply different to the ones spoken by native English people.

Welsh, being the national language of Wales, is spoken there as well as English, as is Irish in Northern Ireland, Scottish Gaelic in the Scottish highlands, Ulster Scots in Ulster and parts of Northern Ireland, and Cornish in the English county of Cornwall. I came to know all these various languages and divides as I related to different people from various parts of the UK. My visit to Cardiff further made me realise how well recognised the Welsh language is, something of which I was formerly unaware. Most words there are written in Welsh but also translated into English.

Another group who have a language different to English are the Cornish people, who are mainly from Cornwall and some parts of Somerset and Dorset. Cornwall, a county in southwestern England, is particularly popular for its Cornish pasties, which are eaten all over the UK. Even though they are part of England, many Cornish people consider themselves not to be English but purely Cornish, with their language attesting to their claim that theirs is a minority language in the UK. Much of their vocabulary is similar to the other Celtic languages of Welsh, Scottish Gaelic, and Irish, and does not in any way sound like English. It sounds rather like Welsh, and their writing is not English at all. The Cornish successfully saw to the New Testament of the *Bible* being translated into Cornish. A visit to Cornwall could help help a person in learning the language, or at least in picking up a few odd words.

Other ethnic-minority languages that are not formally recognised, but are acknowledged, include Caribbean Creole, which may be heard in the East and South ends of London, if nowhere else. Urdu, Punjabi, Bengali, Cantonese Chinese, and Hindi are some of the others. In some areas in the UK, most public services leaflets have translations in some of these languages for easier communication to their speakers, or those whose first language isn't English. I would have thought that anyone living in England would employ English as his or her first language, but I've met individuals who have lived in the UK for decades who cannot communicate in any form of English.

That reminds me of a classmate of mine whom I happened to visit at home. Her family originated from the Middle East, but have been resident in the UK for many years. In spite of her mum living in the UK for over thirty years, she couldn't hold a simple conversation with me in English. Her daughter had to translate everything I said, including simple salutations, for her into their local language.

Apparently, a lot of people like that, mostly women, have little or no contact with the outside world other than with their local ethnic communities, so after living in the West for decades their language skills and lifestyles are no different from those who haven't emigrated out of the Middle East or other country of origin. That seemed a bit hard to believe until I met them, though. How they can live in a country and not get integrated into the culture by learning to speak the local language is certainly beyond me.

Imagine people having access to all the educational resources, language schools, evening classes, and adult learning schemes and never utilising these opportunities, which some deprived people so much crave. They live in the land of supply and surplus, yet in dire lack.

CHAPTER 12

THE REAL DEAL HAS JUST STARTED WITH THE OLDIES

Walking down the streets and being greeted by different people was something, but being stopped mainly by the elderly was another experience altogether. It was almost like I had this special affinity for those elderly people, or senior citizens as they are commonly called. Whenever I waited for the bus at a bustop, it wasn't uncommon to see one of them pulling over and starting a conversation.

Some of the conversations could be interesting and sometimes even historical, but at times they could be draining and boring, especially if I'd had a long day at university. During the time that I commuted to Bradford from Leeds it was almost an everyday affair. The senior citizens would be waiting for their buses, too, and would just want to talk to me especially if I smiled or seemed receptive.

One of them told me in conversation about *Coronation Street*, a soap-opera that had been on TV for over fifty years. I was privileged to hear stories of how life was during and after the Second World War from the oldies. The migration of the Irish into England during the potato famine was another historical story one told me. I doubt if I could have gathered so much useful information if not for the oldies.

I usually left the house around 7.30 am to catch the bus and later the train into Bradford. Most mornings I met an elderly lady named Jane, who eventually became my very good friend, waiting to catch the bus, too. As a sign of courtesy, I would say a hearty good-morning to her and she would respond, but one thing that never ceased to bother me was what this elderly lady was travelling into the city centre for every day at that time.

She looked too old to keep a job, not that she was frail or weak, but her smart dressing with well-applied makeup at 7.30 am beggared explanation. She would talk to me about the weather and life in general. It seems as if the Brits never get enough of discussing the weather, as though the fluctuations are strange or unexpected, even though that's what it's been like all their lives. If there were nothing else to discuss, I could be sure that someone would discuss the weather with me at the bus stop.

After a few days, Jane told me everything about herself and family, and I mean everything – all that there was to her life. It was so strange to me that a lady who knew next to nothing about me was opening up all the details of her life to me like that. At the end of the day, I was only the girl at the bus stop!

After giving me the lowdown of what would be many pages of her CV, her interrogation of me began. The briefer the answers I tried to give her, the more questions I got. Even though she was a lovely old lady, I wished she would lose interest in me. I wasn't brought up to open my personal life to people, even less to strangers, unless needed.

I didn't have to ask my newly found friend why she went into the city every morning. Without being asked she told me that she met up with an old friend of many years, maybe forty or something like that, for coffee every morning. I wondered why people would leave their houses to go to town just to have coffee. I wondered why ordinary coffee could not be drunk in their houses where they could have as many cups as they wished. To travel such a long distance in return for a cup of coffee seemed to be mind-boggling.

Since I didn't want her to ask me any more questions about myself, I decided not to ask. What I didn't understand at the time was that meeting up for coffee or tea was only a way of meeting up to chat or catch up with friends, the drink not being the most important thing. Now that I also leave my house to meet my friends for coffee I can identify with it more.

However, leaving the house could also mean that she could save money on heating it all day. I have heard that senior citizens do that as a means of economising. How ridiculous was that, leaving one's house to go to a coffee house to save money on bills? A lot of the older citizens, whom I feel should stay at home in the winter enjoying themselves, are known to employ this strategy to cut down their bills.

I thought the UK was a place of plenty and surplus. Why do these old people have to be so frugal with their bills? I was starting to question the impression of wealth for all and sundry in the country that was painted in my mind until that time. Whether they couldn't really afford the heating or they were just being tight-fisted was something I could not explain.

Jane and I became better friends as I started talking to her more freely on the bus trips, which took almost an hour every morning. She was indeed an enormously pleasant lady who gave me loads of advice on how to live my life in the UK as a foreign national. One advice that really stuck with me was her advice on money matters and debt.

Being particularly green at the time, I didn't know of the lives millions lived based on loans and credit cards. She advised me not to live my life on credit at all, and to reject all credit-card and loan offers, explaining that I would be enslaved to the banks for most of my life if I did. She said that her husband worked in a bank during his working life and the only loan they ever took out was the mortgage on their property, and that that should be my sole aim throughout my stay in the UK.

Even though I was invited to her house for tea a few times, one thing that stuck to me about her, even as I write, was that advice. If only I'd taken her words on board, that would have been the best help I would have rendered to myself until I was lured into getting a student credit card.

With my African upbringing of showing respect to older folks, I found it difficult to ignore some of the senior citizens who chose to have some not-too-interesting conversations on the bus or at the stop, but did I get some rib-cracking tales to tell. On a particular occasion, I stood at the bus stop waiting for my bus when an elderly man asked if I knew when the bus was due. I answered him and he started a conversation, as usual.

Most of the senior citizens live by themselves, so that the only times they encounter people to relate with or talk to is in public places. This is completely unlike Africa, where the older members of families generally have grandchildren or distant relatives living with them, especially during the last years of their lives.

Anyway, this man appreciated my response and said that he thought that I was a lovely girl. To express that more clearly he started to pull my cheeks. There I was, standing with mixed feelings and unease. Even though I wasn't comfortable with this, I politely moved backwards a bit to get away from this bus stop fan of mine.

As if that weren't enough, he complimented my hair, saying that it looked nice and that he might tell his wife to have the same. Unfortunately, he touched my head, and the hair-extension piece I'd attached to my hair was loosely affixed. I was dead worried it was going to come off embarrassingly in public. What kind of man was this who didn't just pull my cheeks but went as far as touching my hair? I was greatly pleased when he got his hands off my hair while I still had the hairpiece intact and got on the bus. To avoid further scenes, I made my way to the back of the bus while he sat in front. Thank God it was over.

Another scenario with the oldies occurred once when I was in a beauty and cosmetics store examining the products to buy. An elderly (since calling anyone "old" is a taboo in the UK) lady moved over to my side and started one of those usual off-track conversations with me. After making an enquiry on what I was doing in the shop, she decided to give me a proper tutorial as to why a young girl like me shouldn't wear makeup. She continued this pep talk until I was forced to walk out of the store in obedience to her firm instructions.

Respect and honour for older people had been instilled in me from childhood and it was an inherent part of my life. Since I was bored with her words and her strict admonition not to buy or use makeup because, in her estimation, I was too young, I moved out to avoid her and stood by the side waiting for her to leave. As soon as I saw her leave,

I stepped back inside, but this time I vowed to avoid as many senior citizens as I possibly could.

Now that so many old people moved towards me to start conversations, I started to think that maybe I was destined to hang out with the oldies. Good as they were, most of my part-time jobs at university were involved with the care of the elderly, and I enjoyed every bit of them. They could be really amusing, and maybe I'm of the older generation, or what other explanation can I give?

CHAPTER 13

THE REAL STUDENT LIFE; LIVING IN BRADFORD

Getting the right suitable accommodation while studying, especially being away from family and friends, could mean the difference between a fun-filled university life and boredom and depression. Loads of options were available, depending on what exactly I wanted. There were en-suite rooms, bedsits, and single rooms with shared facilities in the university halls of residence.

Some students absolutely loathe the idea of living in the halls, where they share the kitchen and bathroom facilities, and they would rather live with their friends in shared houses, rent their own apartments, or live in as a tenant with a landlord or family. Renting off-campus could be cheaper in some instances, but eventually the bills for such utilities as gas, electricity, water, and telephone could add up so that the cost would be as high as living on the university campus.

Fortunately, students in full-time education don't need to pay any council tax, which could be a whopping amount. Council tax is charged on an annual basis to every household and building in the UK by the local government councils, based on the number of individuals living in the house and the house's value. The more expensive a property is, the higher the council tax classification. The money is said to be used in providing such council services as emptying household wastes and cleaning the roads. Not having to pay that is a thumbs-up for students.

Having lived for my first few weeks with my cousin in Leeds, I commuted from Leeds to Bradford every day, which wasn't too convenient. I later decided to get accommodation closer to the university and went in search of houses near the university campus. As I frantically toured nearby streets, I viewed a number of houses which were mostly terraced, old-looking buildings.

The only problem with house-viewing was getting lost. Bradford's area-naming system is odd. In a designated area, I could find a street named Ashgroove Street; next to it would be Ashgroove Terrace, Ashgroove Lane, Ashgroove Place, Ashgroove Walk, Ashgroove Drive, and Ashgroove Road. If I didn't take particular note of where I had been, it was easy to lose my way and stumble a bit before heading in the right direction.

As I was contemplating living in one of those houses based on its external architecture, which didn't look too impressive, my friend Rebecca and I decided to view the interiors. To our surprise, the interiors of most of the houses were superb, no comparison with their tattered-looking exteriors. We discovered that most of the houses were beautifully designed, magnificent, spacious, and well-decorated on the inside. Some had up to six or eight spacious bedrooms located on up to three or four separate floors. "Whao!" was the exclamation that came from both of us as we walked around those houses. For me, that was the beginning of the discovery of British architecture.

Another surprising element we discovered as we viewed the houses was the friendliness and openness of their residents, who were mainly students, anyway. They opened their doors to us strangers without even questioning our identities, as long as we disclosed that we were students in search of accommodation. They even took us round to inspect the rooms and other domestic facilities, which would be the bases of our price bargains.

These were in contrast to my home country, where we guard our doors with maximum security, build tall fences, and even get barbed wires for security reasons. Here, many houses hardly have fences, and at those that do the fences are only meant to demarcate the property from that of the neighbours and not necessarily to provide security.

Even though I appreciated these gestures, I would not embark on such a house-viewing on my own. It is always advisable to have someone else for company. It's even advisable to notify one's friends during the house-hunting mission, as it is not uncommon to hear of incidents of assault or rape.

After Rebecca and I checked about ten houses, we finally found one which I felt seemed suitable. It had the facilities I wanted and was only about a five-minute walk to the university. It was a Victorian-style building with a two-bedroom apartment on one of the floors.

Rebecca and I had seen the advert of a spare room that had been pasted on the window of the house and we decided to check the property out properly. We rang the bell and waited for about fifteen minutes before a young Chinese lady attended to us at the door. We introduced ourselves and explained our house-hunting mission to her.

The lady introduced herself as Moon. I tried as much as I could to hide my amusement on hearing the name, while Rebecca and I signalled to each other. I chuckled a bit, and when I could no longer hide the emotions I burst into laughter, pretending that the cause of my laughter was the way my friend was looking. I couldn't understand why she answered to the unusual name. This was the beginning of an era of hearing different and strange-sounding names. I started to hear of ladies bearing names I thought were male, like Alex and Sam, which I learnt were only nicknames for Alexandra and Samantha.

Moon took us round to the third floor, where a flat she shared with her younger sister was situated. It was a two-bedroom flat with a spare bedroom for whoever was interested. The room in question was a double bedroom with a single bed placed in the middle and a two-seater sofa located on the left-hand side. The room was plastered with artistic, cream-based, colour wallpaper. It also included a bed-side lamp on the bedside table and an Oakwood wardrobe on the right-hand side. Right beside the wardrobe was a reading table and a chair. The room looked sparkly clean, with burgundy curtains hanging on the wall and a matching carpet on the floor.

I immediately fell in love with the room's lay-out and design. To cap it all off was a newly installed kitchen and bathroom, which was exactly what I wanted. I immediately negotiated the price with Moon, who was actually sub-letting the room to me. The good thing about the arrangement was that she had the landlord's consent. Moon was ecstatic that she and her sister had a flatmate when I decided to take the room up.

The arrangements were all fine, but my curiosity about the origin of the name Moon had in no way dwindled. I was really keen to know whether it was her real name or a nickname. I wasted no time in satisfying my inquisitive mind by asking her.

If hearing the name got me laughing, the explanation she gave as to how the name came about got Rebecca and me reeling in unquenchable laughter. Her Chinese name wasn't Moon and neither is it translated into Moon in English. She said that her mates at college in England gave her the name Moon because the shape of her face was as round as a full moon. The name stuck on her throughout college and she decided to answer to it as long as she stayed in England.

How sarcastic could these classmates of hers be? How terrible was it that they found no name more befitting for the sweet, lovely girl than Moon. Generally, in British society humour is often used as a weapon of sarcasm. If people find it difficult to insult someone directly, the insults are made using humour. Moon's sister was more fortunate, as she was given the name Rachel, a prim and proper name, but what in the world went wrong with Moon? It's a good thing she wasn't given the name Moonie, after all.

As I interacted with many more Chinese students on campus, I realised that it was common for them to bear English names, mostly given to them by their English teachers. Many of them bear such names as Peace, Sarah, or Winnie. They bear such names only in class and not officially. So, don't be surprised to have a Chinese friend by the name Eddie, only to discover on searching for his record that there is absolutely nothing that refers to that name.

One reason why they take English names is because their native names aren't easily pronounceable for English speakers. It's common knowledge that most Brits answer to short forms of their names. British

If hearing the name got me laughing, the explan
gave as to how the name came about got Rebecca and me
unquenchable laughter. Her Chinese name wasn't Moon and neither
is it translated into Moon in English. She said that her mates at
college in England gave her the name Moon because the shape of her
face was as round as a full moon. The name stuck on her throughout
college and she decided to answer to it as long as she stayed in
England.

How sarcastic could these classmates of hers be? How terrible
was it that they found no name more befitting for the sweet, lovely girl
than Moon. Generally, in British society humour is often used as a
weapon of sarcasm. If people find it difficult to insult someone directly,
the insults are made using humour. Moon's sister was more fortunate,
as she was given the name Rachel, a prim and proper name, but what in
the world went wrong with Moon? It's a good thing she wasn't given the
name Moonie, after all.

As I interacted with many more Chinese students on campus,
I realised that it was common for them to bear English names, mostly
given to them by their English teachers. Many of them bear such names
as Peace, Sarah, or Winnie. They bear such names only in class and
not officially. So, don't be surprised to have a Chinese friend by the
name Eddie, only to discover on searching for his record that there is
absolutely nothing that refers to that name.

One reason why they take English names is because their native
names aren't easily pronounceable for English speakers. It's common
knowledge that most Brits answer to short forms of their names. British

people's names tend to be monosyllabic. To an African student like me, some of the names were unusual, especially the abbreviated forms.

Getting back to my newly-found student accommodation, it was all going well until the house's hygiene went off track. What was more, I found something unexpected in the twenty-first-century UK — those tiny creeping creatures. Yes! Mice came creeping around the apartment. How bizarre was that? I was too shocked for words and didn't understand how they got into my room.

At the end of the day, we had to contact the local council for pesticides because chemical substances are tightly controlled in the country for health and safety reasons. Getting pesticides is almost synonymous with climbing the mount of Gibraltar.

With the mice increasing in number, destroying the furniture, and making the apartment messy, Moon wanted to move out of the house. Being a sub-tenant, I had to look for another accommodation within a stressfully short space of time. I didn't seem to get any useful leads via UNIPOL, an organisation that helps with securing off-campus accommodation. They had an office situated on campus and students could navigate the available city apartments via their computer system.

By then, however, the winter season had arrived and daytime activities tended to be reduced, and by the time it was four o'clock the streets were terribly dark. The streets weren't well illuminated and the cold was seriously unbearable. All these factors made house-hunting a bit difficult, and I did not want an accommodation that would be too far from the campus. I wanted a place I could reach easily after spending some extra time in the library.

Bradford. The day after I spoke to her she asked me to follow her to see a house which was only about a fifteen-minute walk from the university campus.

On seeing the house, I was pleased with all the facilities and the weekly rent. I met the landlord, who introduced me to the other three housemates, a lady and two guys. They were all students at the university, too, and appeared welcoming and accommodating.

Having heard so much about student lifestyles, I asked if they weren't into wild late-night parties, smoking, and excessive drinking in the house, because I wanted a place with some peace and quiet. Their response was that even though they all smoked, they tried not to drink excessively to the point of drunkenness in the house. They said that if they were planning to get drunk, they'd usually go out partying.

Since they knew I might not be comfortable with smoking, they promised to smoke outside the house or only when I wasn't cooking in the kitchen. By this time, I was getting used to the binge-drinking and smoking which appear to be a huge part of the UK's youth culture. I could never have imagined how people could get drunk on purpose.

Before they went out for parties, they would have mapped out a plan for getting drunk, since getting drunk on purpose is considered to be fun. Getting drunk and being sick afterwards is almost like a competition at which someone wants to beat the other person. I told them that I neither drink nor smoke, and it was a big surprise to them. They then inferred that I had no fun or enjoyment in my life. As long as I enjoyed my life and got on well with it, I wasn't bothered that I wasn't part of the clique. As if the only connecting bridge to a full, fun-filled student life is drunkenness or wildness.

Anyway, I moved into the house late on Friday night, thinking that I would cope for the few months that I needed the accommodation. We had reached a compromise on their social activities and my conservative lifestyle. If only I knew what was to come afterwards. My good friend Rebecca had helped me in moving some of my things into the new apartment and had left later that night.

It was around 8.00 pm when they started smoking in the kitchen and I was asked to excuse them because they weren't used to smoking outside. I left them to it and retreated into my bedroom, which was the only room on the ground floor. After a few hours, a few more students had arrived in the house; they were having a party. I thought that it might still be fine, since I kept to my room while it was all going on.

By midnight things were getting a bit out off control. They were absolutely drunk, screaming and swearing at the top of their voices. I peeped out of my room and saw the revelling that was going on in the kitchen. The lady in the house saw me, and in her drunken state asked me to join in. I refused and made a speedy retreat back into my room.

The shouting and songs continued, and to make matters worse, people were banging heavily on my door to join in the fun. I was really terrified for my life, because I had never been so close to drunken people in my life, and from the little I knew, a drunken man could do anything in that state, since he has no inhibitions.

All I could do was pray quietly that I would be left alone in peace. When I refused to answer, the lady started screaming that she wasn't drunk and that I should come out to see her. I had no choice then, since the banging had gone on for around twenty minutes. I went out, saw her and told her that I was in agreement that she wasn't drunk. I simply agreed with everything she said at that moment to get away as fast as I could.

It seemed to me that she was even more drunk than any of the guys in the group. What meaningful conversation could I hold with someone who was under the heavy influence of alcohol? All that was in my mind just then was a way to escape. It was my first night in the house, but I knew that I was in for a horrible time from my very sociable neighbours.

That night was one that I will not forget in a hurry. As it went on, I needed to use the toilet, which was on the first floor, but alas, my housemates were sitting on the stairs, screaming and getting sick with vomit. I had no choice than to relieve myself many hours later. What a welcoming experience in my new student house! I just couldn't sleep all night and called my friend Rebecca to help me move my things out the next morning before they woke up. I sensed that once they were sober, they would try to convince me to stay in the house, which would have been difficult for me to cope with.

In all fairness, they seemed to be reasonably nice guys, but I knew that once the victims of alcoholic intoxication are bitten by its uninhibiting venom, every act of niceness would be totally out of the scene. This wasn't what I had planned for and I didn't intend to spend another night under those conditions. It was not too tasking to move again, since my suitcase and bags were still intact; I had only removed my bedding and nightwear for the night.

As early as 7.00 am, Rebecca was there to pack my things into her room in the university hall of residence. Having paid the landlord the deposit and a few weeks rent, I called him to notify him of my decision and how I didn't feel that the house's environment would be conducive for my needs. He tried as hard as he could to convince me that they would refrain from any more drunken sessions and that I would be fine. I flatly refused and insisted that I wanted my rent and deposit back, since I had only spent one night. I thought it was going to be straightforward, but to my dismay he reminded me of the contract I signed on the day I moved in and how it was binding.

I tried pleading with him to consider my plight, but my pleas fell on deaf ears. My best option was to get half the rent back and to lose the deposit. I momentarily felt helpless and like a big fool, since I had truly signed the contract, but at the same time I felt that the landlord wasn't being fair to me.

Part of the contract was to have some peace and quiet in the house and not the wildness I had experienced overnight. I explained my financial situation to him, which was that I didn't have any money to pay for another accommodation, but he just didn't budge a bit. I realised that I had made a mistake which I would have to pay for. The lesson from that was to look well before I leapt next time and to understand that once I had voluntarily signed a contract it was binding.

I didn't know how to tell my parents what had happened to the money, so I had to look for a way out by myself. Rebecca was kind enough to accommodate me in her room for a few days, and she advised me afterwards to take up the university accommodation in the halls of residence.

With no money for the deposit required, I felt trapped, yet I had to move out of my friend's room. I did get a way out in the end by applying for a small loan from the university's Student Financial and Information Service (SFIS), which offered me a £200 loan without interest and gave me a few months to pay it back. That money bailed me out of my self-inflicted predicament. I was extremely grateful to the university for providing such a support system. What would I have done at that time? Thank God! I sailed through the odds.

THE REAL CHASE INTO THE UNIVERSITY HALL

With the deposit paid, I was allocated a room in Longside Hall on campus. It was a single study room with basic amenities: a reading table and chair, a single bed and mattress placed in the left-hand corner, a wardrobe, a bookshelf hanging over the reading table and chair, a wash basin placed next to the wardrobe, and a red carpet laid on the floor.

The rooms are arranged into tiny flats, with each flat comprised of four study rooms. We had two bathrooms and toilets to share between the two flats. The room looked much nicer and neater than the two student houses I had previously stayed in and getting to meet various students was another advantage to it. The electricity, water, and gas bills were all included in the rent, which made life a lot easier too. I settled well into the hall and had lovely hall mates this time around.

We had two large kitchens, with dining sets for the twenty-four students, fridges, freezers, and storage cupboards for our use. The problem with the cupboards, fridges, and freezers was that they were occupied on a first-come-first-served basis, so someone like me, who resumed into the hall mid-semester, had to use the least space available. It was okay because I had reasonable and decent hall mates, and those I shared the kitchen with were easy-going ones.

As I settled into the hall of residence, I discovered that mine was indeed an international block. We had like four English students and Malaysian, Chinese, Polish, and Dutch nationals. It made the place livelier and I had the chance to learn other countries' cultures and cuisines, as sometimes we shared our different foods and delicacies. It was real fun living among these students. At least there were no wild parties and drunken sessions. I was also availed the opportunity of learning my hall mates' different traditions and attitudes.

When it was down to cooking, most of them commented on how long it took for my African dishes to be made in contrast to the English mates, who ate microwave and ready-made food most of the time. I was forced to ask them at one stage whether English people had any dishes that had to be prepared from scratch.

The Chinese students, on the other hand, hardly ate any ready-made food. Their ways of life as students were highly commendable.

For them, meal times were like celebrations. They would take their time, cooking many dishes at the same time, but most of those dishes were usually vegetables. It was surprisingly different from the Chinese meals we have in restaurants. It was interesting that they hardly ever ate with forks and knives or spoons, preferring instead to use their traditional chopsticks.

To show how serious the Chinese students were with their cooking, each of them had brought a portable rice cooker from home, so when I walked into our kitchen I'd find about six rice cookers going at a time. It wasn't a problem for anyone initially until all of them started using their rice-cookers at the same time, which threw the circuit breaker which served the cookers, microwave, and fridges. We other students had to forfeit our chances of cooking for the day. It wasn't until we got the university electrician involved that we got the matter rectified.

The Dutch and Polish students were on an ERASMUS exchange placement and had their own special dishes as well. They did a bit of cooking and had their ready-made meals, too. Even though I never witnessed them drunk throughout their stay in the hall, their usual drinks were vodka and gin. If I thought having many bottles or cans of lager could be an issue, I saw bigger volumes of vodka and spirits being taken at once, yet I never saw them intoxicated. It was tolerable as long as they weren't into antisocial behaviour in public.

Generally, it was fun living in the halls of residence because everyone had to abide by the university's rules and regulations. Although the rent for the halls could be slightly higher than living off campus, the benefits were numerous and worthwhile.

Apart from the security of living in a student community with security wardens on patrol, we had cleaners who took care of our toilets, bathrooms, and kitchen on weekdays. There was also the exposure to other cultures and the chance to interact with students from various countries. I had friends with different courses and backgrounds, which was good in broadening my horizons. No amount of money could buy those aspects of education.

To crown it all, I could stay in the university library till late and get to my room at any time safely. The socialisation that the halls of residence availed me was so precious that missing out of it would have been a loss. I would recommend that any first-year international student live in the university halls. It not only helps in settling down into the new life and getting a real feel of the flow of events, it also helps in beating the home-sickness syndrome that comes with living in a foreign country. Getting to meet fellow international and home students and fostering great friendships are parts of the educational experience that should not be missed.

Of course, there were the challenges of living with people with different personalities and attitudes. The boys especially found cleaning up surfaces after them difficult and left most of their crockery in the sink. Could it be that they were expecting some fairy domestic goddesses to sort them out? They cleaned up when someone spoke to them, though, but that could be a bit irritating at times.

We had issues with items going missing in the communal kitchen areas, and at times with food items going missing from the fridges. Even though we could only gain access into the hall with electronic swipe cards, the security wasn't an absolute hundred percent.

A few months into living in the halls my electric blender went missing. I didn't notice this until one of my hall mates needed it. It was bulky and inside its pack, so it was difficult to imagine that someone could have walked into the hall, picked it up, and made away with it without being challenged. I asked everyone in the hall, but no one had a clue as to where or how the blender had disappeared. I was pretty sure it didn't grow legs or wings on its own accord, though. I never found it, but when I finally got it replaced I stored the new one securely inside my bedroom.

As necessary, I reported the theft to the accommodation authorities, but little could be done to address the situation at that stage. We were always advised to keep our property as safe as possible and not to allow unknown people into the hall. Whatever happened to my blender and other missing items is still a mystery. Burglars are known to operate in students' accommodations because they believe that many students don't consider the issue of security to be important. It's partly true, as one is usually overly security-confident and maybe a bit carefree when living among fellow students.

An interesting part of living with different nationals was learning a few words of their languages and breaking down the communication barrier. Since most of us in that hall didn't speak English as out first language, it was a bit challenging to pass across messages explicitly in English. Sign language, electronic translators, and gesticulations were some of our communication tools.

One of the Polish hall mates was trying to tell me what she'd learnt in her English class (they were offered English classes in addition to their normal course of study), and I didn't quite grasp what she was explaining clearly. Apparently, she had mentioned a word that sounded like 'lawn' but had actually meant to say 'lion'. Since I didn't understand her, she roared heavily at me and said, "That animal." It was such an hysterical performance that I couldn't help laughing uncontrollably at the communication gaps we were trying to deal with.

Then, there were the strange things I learnt living in halls, such as being laughed at for visiting the laundrette fortnightly. I was told that students only do their washing twice in a semester – the mid-term break and at the end of the semester when they had to go home for holidays. True, many students would wear the same pair of jeans almost forever before it ever got a thorough cleaning. I didn't subscribe to that idea and appeared unstudently for washing too frequently. The laundrette was located a few metres from the hall and required a few coins to use, so I didn't see the stress in using it as much as I needed.

Some of my flatmates did not shower daily. I had observed that most mornings, the bathroom I shared with three other girls in a flat-like section was always dry, meaning that nobody had used it before me. Surprisingly, they would be fully dressed and ready to go before I got ready for classes. I was determined to know their secrets because I couldn't understand what was going on.

At least I knew that the rooms weren't en-suite, so they must have had alternative methods every morning. So I got into a conversation about how they got dressed very early in the morning and how they never waited on me to use the bathroom. To my amused discovery, they didn't use any alternative bathroom but used the wash basin located in each room and a flannel to get washed. That's one alternative to having a bath or shower, I reckon. It was such a shock to believe that someone could go out into a day without having a shower. I was living in the real student world.

CHAPTER 14

TAKE ME BACK HOME, I'M TERRIBLY HOMESICK

By the time I had spent about two months in the hall I started to feel heavily homesick. I did not have the kind of university life I had previously had in Nigeria, and was seriously longing for that. I had heard people talk about homesickness, but couldn't believe that I would ever be a victim of the syndrome. Everything felt too lonely. Except for the few Nigerian friends and classmates I had, no one visited me in the hall, and to visit anyone I had to make a firm arrangement first. I was used to people popping around impromptu, not these religiously formal procedures adhered to in the UK.

It first started with just going to classes and returning back to the hall each day, with all my hall mates minding their own business. Then my friend Rebecca crossed over to another university in London due to some personal issues, which meant I was on my own most of the time. The close friendship we had developed in such a short space of time had been strained by the distance. The nostalgic feelings for Nigerian student life, the friends I'd had, and our social and faith-based events, things which were either missing or not the same in the UK, further contributed to my homesickness.

At first, I tried battling the syndrome by writing extensive narrative letters to my many friends and read their replies over and over again. I spent a lot of my meagre pocket money on making international calls, but realised that nothing could simply replace the hole within.

I lost my appetite for real food and got myself hooked on chocolate bars as a way of coping until I became a Kit-Kat addict, piling up the calories on the way, too. All I wanted was to get out of the strange and foreign system.

In spite of the sophistication and high level of formal education that I was receiving, I felt like I had lost my entire life and existence. If I wasn't on the phone to folks in Nigeria, I would be lamenting heavily over the phone to my mum, who resided in London. It got to a stage that all I could do was weep without end. I'd had enough of the UK.

When my weeping sessions didn't help matters, I asked to go back to my former university in Nigeria, explaining that I didn't want to be in the UK anymore. I missed the bubbly, exuberant, and friendly Nigerian atmosphere. Here in the UK, people are not that friendly. They could be cold one day, the next day be cheerful, and the day after, act depressed. I had read about the reserved British nature, but was now experiencing it first hand. I just didn't know what to expect. People can be so negative despite most things in the system working. Some of the issues being moaned about would make me cringe. Maybe people just needed to take a look at other nations and get to appreciate how much they had at their disposal.

My mum and family tried as much as they could to comfort and encourage me, but no amount of words from them seemed to help me. I feel that another contributory factor to my homesickness was that I was juggling a part-time job with full-time studying. I'd never had to hold a job down when I was in Nigeria, but in the UK I had to in order to augment my pocket money. I thought that it would be fun working and having the feeling of taking some responsibility for my life. Alas! It was a joke.

As the situation continued, my mum suggested that I change my university to one in London; maybe living close to family would help matters. That sounded like the perfect solution to the problem, which was taking a great toll on my countenance and wellbeing. So I contacted a few universities in London, and fortunately for me I was offered a place at the London Metropolitan University subject to getting a release from the University of Bradford.

I found it difficult to believe that it could be so easy crossing from one university to another, especially since all the enquiries I made were via the telephone and e-mail. At the end of the day, the university authorities treat us students like customers, but why would they want to turn away customers that meet the criteria?

Without much ado, I contacted my departmental head and personal tutor and explained my situation to them. They were wonderfully understanding, even though they tried to encourage me to stay on the course because of the university's international reputation, but I wasn't interested in all that. I knew that the lecturers meant well for me and for the total wellbeing of their students. Needless to say, I was more than appreciative for their support, but all I wanted was to be happy, and if that meant being close to my family, that, it was going to be.

Even though my department had approved my move, the next hurdle that I needed to cross was getting a clearance from the student registry. The main woman in charge of international students was a firm, straight-talking, and sometimes rude woman who would not hesitate to give students a tough time if the need be, especially when it came to the issue of tuition-fee payments. Her name was Mrs Jefferson.

I approached Mrs Jefferson and explained my position to her with the idea of receiving a partial refund of the fee I had paid. She said that it wasn't a problem to cross over as I had intended, but that only a tiny proportion of the fees, maybe a third, could be refunded back to me since I had received lectures and some study materials in the class for about three months. I left her office in a frustrated state, feeling that she was being plain unfair; at least I had not sat for the first semester exams. The amount in question that I had to forfeit would be a few thousand pounds, which wasn't peanuts that I could ignore.

Knowing that I could not convince Mrs Jefferson to agree to a higher partial refund, my parents' decision was to stay on the course and to adjust to the new system. Even though I wasn't pleased with Mrs Jefferson, her stand, which hindered my move to London, turned out to be a real blessing in disguise. I would have missed out on the exciting times that I had later on at the university. Everything truly worked together for my good in the end.

In combating my homesickness, I became more socially active on purpose. I joined societies and a xtian group: "Students of the word" who met every Monday evening for meals and times of fellowship. My time at the students of the word group introduced me to a number of English cuisines, like mashed potatoes, cottage pie, beef hotpot, and curries. I got used to the dishes and learnt to embrace different cultures as well.

In that period I also met many other Nigerian students, and before the session came to a close we formed a society called the Diaspora Association of Nigerian Students. I became the publicity secretary. It was great meeting up regularly with fellow-minded students and sharing our strange experiences in a foreign country. Getting to laugh at one another, giving and receiving counsel on how to cope with UK university life, challenging one another academically, and knowing that I had a support group were indispensable assets I received from the group. Before I knew it, I felt very much at home in Bradford and started to enjoy every bit of my stay.

One of the Nigerian students spoke of his experience in the hospital when he came down with a bout of malaria. He was referred to the hospital and was given what in his opinion was "special treatment". He had one-to-one barrier nursing and was confined to a private room. What he didn't realise at the time was that he was being quarantined and kept away from all other patients, whom they didn't want to be infected.

Malaria is treated like leprosy in the UK, and because of the harm posed to the public; patients suffering from it are given the type of isolated treatment which he classified as special. According to him, his main problem while in hospital was that he didn't have access to any African or Nigerian food until a Nigerian doctor came along. Coupled with the so-called special treatment, he also got a special home-cooked meal from the doctor.

CHRISTMAS CELEBRATION

In December we had our first-term break for Xmas. I went down to London to see my family and friends. What I realised was that the way Xmas is celebrated in the UK is sharply different to the way we celebrate in Nigeria.

A few months before Xmas, like October or November, the shops were filled with festive items and gifts for family and loved ones. People spend an absolute fortune on buying Xmas gifts and often get into debt in the process. As far as people in the UK are concerned, Xmas is simply a time to exchange expensive gifts and probably to meet family members who have not been contacted throughout the year. How strange is it that some people don't contact their family members throughout the year, when they might need them the most, but shower expensive gifts on them at Xmas time.

It appears as though the essence of the celebration has been lost in the euphoria of exchanging expensive material items. It is normally about the Christmas gift each child in the family wants and how the parents have to get those items, which at times is out of convenience.

A traditional Xmas celebration would be on a cold, wintry December afternoon with a meal of roast turkey, roast potatoes, vegetables, and cranberry sauce as an accompaniment. Lots of chocolates, biscuits, and sweet treats are part of the celebration. It's a season when many people pile up the calories, only to shed them a few weeks later in the gym and on diets. It seemed totally different to my known celebration of Xmas, in which people distribute food and drinks to their neighbours and friends.

On the d-day, some family friends invited my sister and me over to their house to celebrate Xmas with them. Unknown to me, there was no public transport available, and even taxis had to be pre-booked to get the service. Of course, double the normal fares are charged on Xmas day. It looked extremely quiet and dead boring on the streets.

People stay indoors with their families and hardly visit one another on Xmas day, contrary to the exuberant celebrations we have in Nigeria, where we'd visit different families and friends freely. Gifts might be exchanged, but not with the pomp and pageantry that is displayed in the UK.

The Xmas holiday helped me to get over my terrible homesickness for a while, but I still missed Nigeria terribly. I wanted the feel of the extended family and local community which I once was used to.

BACK TO UNIVERSITY

On returning to university in January, I got back to my studies and hall life. My hands were getting fuller with a close social circle and a part-time job which I got just before Xmas. The session went on rapidly, with the Easter break the only holiday we had between January and summer.

The summer season had arrived towards the end of that academic session and it was splendid. I had been waiting so long for the sun, having endured so many harsh winter months. All over campus, people were more alive, friendly, and exuberant. Even the colours of the clothes people wore showed how invigorating the presence of the sun could be.

However, that meant more booze and day-time parties. It was a carnival-like setting, especially at the end of the exam period. The student union and other student societies organised various gigs and events in the open places. We had a well-groomed open grass field known as the amphitheatre where everyone relaxed. It was really an exciting time. It was as though the season should never end, without the sickening drunken sessions, of course.

At the end of the session, my hall mates and I organised a barbeque get-together as a parting event for the Erasmus students and the graduating students. It was fun, with loads of food, nibbles, and drinks. Others might have been celebrating the end of exams, graduation, or other events, but mine was a thanksgiving for feeling the sun once again as I had in Nigeria. I had a feel of my homeland's weather and the feeling was ecstatic. For once I enjoyed partying the student way.

Even though I enjoyed my stay in the mixed-gender hall, the bit of messiness, mainly on the part of the boys, had discouraged me from living in a mixed hall. To avoid that, I applied for a university accommodation in an all-female hall for the next year. I thought that ladies would be more hygienic, and they would be more peaceful overall. How wrong was I? That decision almost cost me my sanity with the female neighbour from Hell that I had in my final year.

SUMMER JOB INTERVIEW

By the end of my first academic session in Bradford I was getting much more settled and was looking forward to spending the summer holiday in the area. There were so many summer jobs that were advertised and targeted mainly at students. One was Camp America, where one could work with children and teenagers in summer camps in the United States. Unfortunately, I wasn't recruited for the job.

Other opportunities came up within the Bradford area and I applied as usual. A particular summer job was working with different charity organisations to raise funds and to seek for sponsors. I could be assigned to raise funds for Cancer Research UK, the Children in Need charity, or Oxfam. The prospect of raising funds and awareness for such causes was highly motivational. I was keen on putting my best foot forward at the interview in order to get the job.

Good as it was, the interview was scheduled to take place in Sheffield, about ninety minutes away from Bradford on the coach. I was keenly enthusiastic about attending the interview, and on the d-day I set out early in the morning. The interview was scheduled for 10.00 am at the Sheffield Hallam University. Sheffield being an unfamiliar arena, I left my house as early as 6.30 am to catch the coach at the interchange. On arriving at the venue, I had around an hour to wait for the interview. Little did I know that a large number of students had been called for the interview, so the interviewer did not attend to me till around 11.30 am.

By the time it was my turn to be interviewed, I was already tired and bored from waiting endlessly, but it was my turn at last, and I had resolved to make the best impression ever with the interviewer.

Interestingly, the interview session was going on smoothly until I yawned and stretched myself as the man asked me questions. The young man momentarily stopped and asked if he had bored me with his session.

"Oh! No!" was my quick response, and I tried explaining that I had woken up a bit earlier than usual that particular morning. I further explained that I was just a bit tired having sat on a spot for so long waiting for the interview. It was obvious that my explanations held no water with the man as he gazed at me with an unconvinced look. As far as I was concerned, yawning is a reflex reaction which I had little or no control over. A few minutes after my extensive yawn, the interview was over and I left.

At the time, I didn't think for once that yawning and stretching at an interview would have posed any problem. It wasn't until I told my friends and family that I was told the implication of my action. They unanimously informed me that I should not expect a good outcome from the interview. How truer could my folks' verdict be? I was plainly denied the job. Sadly but funnily, I lost the job I really looked forward to doing.

On the other hand, I did not regret not having that job when I saw many students on the high streets and city centres working in the terrible heat of the summer. The processes that were involved in getting members of the public interested in the various charity organisations were harrowing and, I can imagine, frustrating. Even when I was approached by some of the young workers, I felt as though I was being pestered and harassed for donations. Alas! My yawn and stretch paid off. That wouldn't have been the right job for me

CHAPTER 15
A HOUSE AND A HALF

I took a year out for my student placement, which was in the Bradford area, but lived with a friend of mine named Andrea in a rented house close to the university. Even though I was on placement, I still wanted to be close to the university. We rented from an Indian landlord who seemed to be nicely helpful and friendly at the outset.

Actually, I realised that most of the student houses in Bradford are owned by Indian or Pakistani landlords. We checked the house and thought that it would be ideal for the two of us, but unknown to us our newly rented apartment had many flaws and faults. The landlord assured us that most of the repairs would be made before we moved in and we felt that it was okay.

On moving into the house, however, we realised that the central heating system wasn't working and the window which we thought was double glazed was only single glazed, meaning that the house would be extremely cold during the winter. The shower wasn't functional, which meant that we had to get a bucket and bowl for our daily showers. If that wasn't bad enough, we realised that the washing machine and the tumble dryer were both broken, the kettle was bad, the toaster was rusty, and the television was blurry.

By the time we discovered all these we had already signed the tenancy agreement and had moved into the house. There was no turning back and there wasn't much we could do. The house was horribly cold and damp. Imagine coming from the chilly weather outside and entering into a freezing house. The gas fire that was in the sitting room took something like twenty minutes to put on because it was old and not working properly.

We complained about all these to the landlord, who always had a ready-made answer for every complaint raised. He was a smooth-tongued man who seemed to think he could fix even the most complicated problems with his eloquent speeches. I wonder why politics wasn't his choice of career. It was either he was going to fix it soon or he would engage the services of another person. Hardly did he ever keep to his words, though. At one stage he brought us two electric heaters, which made our electricity bills soar like nobody's business. The house was an absolute nightmare.

We had a welcoming shock during the first week of moving into the house. There was a power cut at around 10 pm on our fourth night there. It was still a bit okay for me to handle, since I had experienced power failures many times in Nigeria, but my Irish friend, who wasn't used to power cuts, had a more distressing time.

It was terrific, but we bailed ourselves out by using our mobile phones to navigate our way around the house, and we were able to get some matches and a candle for illumination. What happened was that Mr Gamal had told us at the point of moving in that there was enough electricity token on the charge card, which we assumed would be okay for at least the first week. We had to run off to a supermarket near the university to top up the electricity credit at that time of night.

If these ordeals weren't horrific enough, we had many more to deal with. The house next to ours was a dilapidated building, which we later learnt was a crack house for drug addicts. Our house was the last on the terrace and that part of the street wasn't well lighted. Some of our neighbours across the street were a group of young men who came across like drug addicts. It wasn't unusual to see them break the windows of their house or gain entrance into the house via a broken door or window.

Our neighbours got high at times and would scream so loud that we heard them in our bedrooms. On one particular occasion I came back from work and couldn't gain entrance into the house, as Andrea had locked it up and was hiding in her bedroom upstairs in a frightened state. One of the guys on the street had seemed to be high and had stood at our door banging incessantly, but not with the intention of entering, anyway. She explained this to me later, and also how she had locked the door so securely that I couldn't get in even with my keys.

We just knew that we were living in the wrong end of town, and worse still in a derelict building. We were two young ladies who needed our peace, but we had to strive extremely hard to have it. We always wondered how we found ourselves in such a terrible situation. We would have done better checking out the area and street properly before moving into the house. I'm sure we could have checked to know what was working properly and what was not before signing the tenancy agreement, to which we had to give a minimum of six weeks notice before it could be terminated.

After making a number of telephone calls, Mr Gamal came around to fix the shower, but kept assuring us about fixing the other things, which he never did. We knew that we had to bear with the situation until we found another one. As time went by, we adjusted to the place. We made our residence an abode and tried as much as we could to enjoy ourselves. All this time, I was on student placement with a scientific company in Shipley, a few miles away from Bradford.

That particular house came with too much baggage. Last but worst of all were the mice that came into our house in their numbers from the dilapidated building next door, feasting on the food in our kitchen and destroying it. Again, we informed the landlord, who made piles of promises to deal with the issue but did nothing. At last, Andrea had to get in touch with the council environmental department, who promised to give us some rat poison. It was scary living with big-sized mice which moved freely around, especially at night time.

One night Andrea woke me up with a loud scream. Alas! It was a mouse that had been caught alive in the mouse trap that the landlord had given to us. She didn't know what to do, with it being alive and so scared. I didn't know what to do either, since we couldn't leave the mouse forever in the trap, but rather than stand there in a state I summoned up courage and hit the tiny creature with a shoe.

Voila! That did the job, but lifting it out into the bin was the most difficult part of the task. With our shrill and scary noises, we eventually wrapped the mouse up and got it out of the house. We'd had more than enough of the house, but still braved it out for a few more months.

Even though the house was in a state, living in a private house with a friend had a number of advantages. We had our space and privacy a bit, and the company we provided for each other was great. I learnt so many things about British and Irish cultures, which was unbeatable.

Quite all right, I knew that Irish people loved their potatoes, being their main staple food, but I wasn't ready to eat potatoes three times every day of the week. Hardly was there a day that she didn't eat potatoes at least twice a day. She would eat potato cakes and hash browns as part of her breakfast, mashed potatoes or chips for lunch, and jacket potatoes or potato wedges for dinner.

It was almost unbelievable the number of times she ate potatoes. Whenever I mentioned it, her explanation was always that she was Irish and that's the way it is in her country of origin. She could say the same of me when it came to the number of rice dishes I ate every week. If only food grows on people, I would have grown some rice grains while she would have grown many tubers of potatoes.

My friend being British and me being Nigerian, we had different interpretations to words or ideas and some of hers were a bit queer for me to get around. Whenever we went out together, people often asked if we lived together, to which I always responded in the positive, but she was always quick to disagree with me, saying that we were house mates and not living together. To me, living together and being house mates were one and the same, so why make the differentiation to people? It didn't make much sense to me until she explained that people asking if we lived together could mean that they assumed that we were in a relationship as homosexual lovers or partners.

I couldn't believe that that idea could be presumed by any right-thinking person. At the end of the day, this was the UK. I grew up in a society where homosexuality is frowned at and not accepted as a norm in life, so the idea was totally weird to me. I learnt quickly and always responded afterwards that we didn't live together but were house mates, after all. I was still learning and realising that I now lived in the UK.

It was funny that although the house denied us many facilities, the landlord would demand the rent even before the due dates, so we were constantly harassed with his calls when the month was running to an end. By the time I finished my student placement, it was time to resume back into university for my final year.

I had learnt how to look and investigate an area properly before moving into a house and what to look for when renting a property. Double glazed windows to keep the heat inside were a must, as were efficient heating and a reliable electricity supply. More importantly, to read the words in small print before signing any tenancy agreement.

Another option with renting a house would have been to check with landlords who were registered with the university authorities or an organisation called UNIPOL, which helps students with their accommodations. Any property registered with UNIPOL would have passed the basic criteria for conducive living so that the landlord could not rip students off easily.

DIY SKILLS: DO IT YOURSELF

While living in the house with Andrea, I learnt a lot about DIY, which had been mostly unknown to me. Back in Nigeria we are not used to the DIY syndrome, whereby people have to carry out most of the household maintenance, carpentry, lighting, bricklaying, and plumbing by themselves. If anything needed fixing, all I was used to doing was employing the services of the appropriate tradesperson. In Nigeria we hardly have to get down to these tasks around the house ourselves, but that is not the case in the UK.

Here in the UK, DIY is generally the option unless the task is a bit complex. The first time someone mentioned DIY, I didn't understand what it meant, so I asked and it was fully explained to me. Even some shops are described as DIY shops, but for a stranger like me it meant nothing. Electricians, plumbers, and carpenters in the UK are not unskilled labourers, as they must have qualifications in those areas and charge their fees according to their skills and qualifications.

Their charges are often so high that DIY is always the cheap option for those people who cannot afford them. Before these people even attend to a problem their customers have to pay a calling-out charge, which could be as high as £200, and rectifying the problem could cost the same amount. Most people therefore learn DIY. Numerous books and guides are sold in shops to offer assistance and help with DIY around the house.

Since I wasn't into DIY, my housemate Andrea, being British, did all the DIY tasks while I offered what little help that I could. Andrea duly dealt with most of the tasks, like changing light bulbs or dealing with electrical appliances, but I watched her doing them to learn the few I could. I doubt if I can call myself a DIY expert, but at least I have learnt a lot and definitely know more than when I lived in Nigeria. Any student who chooses a private accommodation rather than living in the halls needs to be prepared for a bit of DIY, especially if they are unfortunate to have a landlord like ours was.

STUDENT PLACEMENT

The student placement was part of the degree programme, scheduled for a year after the completion of the second year at university. I was a bit reluctant in taking the year out, but all the same I applied to various hospital and commercial laboratories for a position as a laboratory technician or assistant. After sending out a number of applications and receiving no positive responses, I gave up the hope of being a placement student.

During the summer holidays I had begun making preparations to return to university for my final year when I received a telephone call from a scientific company. They had received my application a couple of months earlier and called to confirm if I could attend an interview a week before resuming at university. This was two weeks before the resumption time. In my mind, I had no chance for a placement, but here I was being called for an interview so close on. To make things better, it was in the Bradford area.

I attended the interview, which was more like an informal chat about why I had chosen the company. The interviewer was a recent graduate of my university, so we had a great time discussing how things run in the laboratory and how the experience could help me in my final year of study and career choices in future. She mentioned that she had never conducted an interview before. That gave me a deep sigh of relief, since she seemed relaxed with the whole process. I liked the environment and the work undertaken, but wasn't sure if I really wanted to have the optional year-long placement or not. She offered me the job at the end of the interview, but I requested a few days to decide whether to accept or reject the offer.

I decided to consult some of my lecturers at the university before giving a response to Laura, the company's laboratory manager. I first spoke with my personal tutor, Dr Grisham, who advised me to take the offer, as it would boost my performance in my final year and it would give me the hands-on experience that I so much needed. The head of department corroborated what Dr Grisham said, and added that the experience would make me much more employable after graduation. Some other lecturers said the same.

After all the consultations, I decided to take up the offer, which was really advantageous. It was a real booster to my knowledge base, practical skills, and confidence. I guess a number of students who decided not to have the optional placements didn't know how useful the opportunity is. Earning a reasonable amount of money even made it more appealing and sensible, too.

It was a family-owned-and-run industrial and commercial microbiology company. The chairman, Dan, who had founded the company, was a nicely friendly and down-to-earth man. Even though he had retired from running the company, other than overseeing things as the chairman, he kept himself occupied with a photography studio which was situated on the company premises. He was in his early seventies at the time, but had the habit of seeing to the welfare of all the members of staff.

I could just tell that he was a businessman to the core as he asked me different questions. He took pictures of some of the staff. In no time, I was his good pal and had various picture poses taken without charge. His photography was only a hobby with which he partook in different competitions, and he placed some of the pictures that he took of me were on display in the competitions. It was a two-way affair. He had some portraits for the display of his expertise while I got the portraits for free.

Most of the people I worked with in that laboratory were very warm and friendly. They were ever willing to help whenever I asked for it. To show my appreciation, I bought the scientists some small gifts and cards at Christmas. I placed them on their desks, but observed that for a while no one touched any of the gifts. At last, the manager took hers and asked if I had placed them there. You'd have thought I had presented parcel bombs to them when each of them took the gift.

Many more questions followed, such as "What is this?", "Why are you giving us gifts?", and "How much have you spent on these?" After answering the myriad unbelievable questions, I walked away feeling like a big fool for being generous and nice. Eventually, some of them gave me these cold and suspicious appreciations. It was almost like I had committed a heinous crime by offering those Xmas gifts.

The first person I told of the cold reception I got was my British friend, whom I felt might understand their attitudes better than I did. After narrating my ordeal to her, she explained that in Britain people hardly give Xmas gifts to anyone but family members. In a workplace situation like mine, giving gifts could be interpreted as an attempt to seek favours or to be in the boss's good books.

I couldn't believe my ears and wondered what favour I could be seeking with cheap and simple gifts. With time, I realised that in this society, people are usually sceptical of giving or receiving gifts without definite explanations or occasions. Once I understood the reason behind the coldness, I never offered anyone in the laboratory any gift again.

Even offering to buy someone a meal or drink could be received with suspicion. I would be questioned if I was sure that I really wanted to offer the help and exactly why I wanted to. That was another culture shock to me. My generous African spirit led me to try to show of my appreciation. As far as I was concerned, it was the heart behind the gift rather than its cost that counts most.

Something I observed was that people are relatively tight-fisted in this society, at least compared to the one I grew up in. Hardly would I find people parting with gifts costing as much as £10 unless an occasion warranted it. Even sparing a few quid isn't common, so someone giving freely would be treated with suspicion.

Having lived in the system for a few years now, I think I understand why generosity isn't the normal way of life. Since the government bends people's hands backwards in giving with or without their permission in the name of various taxes, people just want to hold on to the left-over from their hard-earned incomes.

I've heard many people say that they are not interested in giving to charity because the tax they pay is already a way of giving back into society and charity. It's understandable, considering the amount Britons have to pay in tax. Besides the income tax, which is usually around twenty-two percent, they pay council tax, value added tax (VAT), vehicle excise duty, otherwise known as road tax, and to cap them all is the inheritance tax on inherited property.

Of course, the UK also has the stealth taxes, which are dressed up with names like the National Insurance contributions and television license fees. I found it difficult to believe that people have to pay a yearly fee to watch their own televisions sets, but that's just the way it works. I am so grateful that the government has not yet demanded a breathing tax. By the time Britons are through with paying the up-front taxes and the back-handed ones, they're naturally tempted to keep all they have left just to themselves.

Although the placement was challenging, it was boring at times, too, especially when there wasn't much to do. Testing food products and animal feed for the presence of micro-organisms was a bit of fun for my inquisitive self, but examining the microbes wasn't too pleasant at times. Part of my duties involved showing the equipment for sale to customers who came from around the world for viewings. It was all okay until I had to carry out a research project at the end of my training.

My project was to culture various bacteria that would be useful in the food and pharmaceutical industries and to store them viably until they were needed. I thought that with my scientific skills it shouldn't have been a problem, since I had all the support I needed from the senior members of staff, until my manager asked me to collect faeces from everyone in the laboratory. I did as I was instructed, even though it was a bit funny that our bacterial cultures would come from the staff. Even though some of them were a bit reluctant, we got there in the end.

Funnily enough, some of the samples were insufficient and I was forced to ask them for more faecal samples. Imagine having to ask your colleagues for their faeces, knowing who might have supplied the specimen. Although the samples were supplied anonymously, it still seemed queer working tirelessly with my colleagues' samples. That and documenting which bacteria was found in each subject sample were the embarrassing parts of the project. It was all part of the fun and excitement of being a scientist-in-training.

By the time I was rounding off the placement, it was time to resume back into university for the final year. The feeling of being away from serious academic work was there, but the euphoria of living among students came along, too. I just loved the academic environment so much that I wanted to get back. Of course, I was going to move out of Mr Gamal's house back to the university halls of residence. Final year, here I come!

THE REAL NEIGHBOUR FROM HELL

At last I resumed back for my final year. I had secured a room in the university hall, so I moved in during the first week of resumption. A few of my friends had taken places in the hall, too, so having suitable company wasn't an issue. This time around I was in a female-only hall because I thought that it would be cleaner, tidier, and much more peaceful.

All of a sudden, I had mostly brand-new classmates, since most of my former classmates had graduated while I was on placement. Having to befriend new mates, form study groups, and get used to new faces were the few prices to pay for the placement year. Fortunately, one of my neighbours in the hall of residence was a classmate. It made studying and getting along a lot easier.

One evening, I realised that a female student had moved in and her family had come to help in sorting her things out. That gave me an impression that my next door neighbour would be a reasonable type from a responsible family. From the way she and her family dressed, they appeared to be strict Muslims. That was exactly what I had envisaged before moving in: living with responsible and decent female students.

It wasn't a week after Asher moved in that the three of us in that flat knew that we were in for plenty of trouble. Most of her guests were male students who wouldn't leave till the early hours of the morning, so that none of us could move around freely in our nightwear in the hall. It wasn't unusual for a minimum of six to nine people to be in her room at any given time.

They would chat at the top of their voices, scream, and play music full blast, so that the hall mates from the other flats were becoming disturbed, too. Unfortunately for me, she was directly next door to me. After getting drunk, they would scream and run down the stairs in a berserk manner. Even though other hall mates were being affected, I bore most of the brunt of her crazy actions.

She would get so excited and high that she would shout my name from her room, asking how I was doing, and at times this could be as early as 6.00 am. When it first started, I would plead with her and her friends to keep their volume down, as I was in my final year and needed to study. She never hesitated to tell me that she had paid her accommodation fees the same as I had and that she had the right to do as she liked.

Asher was a real neighbour from hell. When it got to the point of her slamming her legs against the wall that separated our rooms and slamming her wardrobe room, I suspected she was under the influence of something more than alcohol – drugs, maybe.

As it was, I worked some night shifts on my part-time job, but found it extremely difficult to catch any sleep on my return in the morning. I often went to another friend's room after my night shifts. All the other hall mates were fed up with her as well. As often as two to four times a week we were forced to call out the security officers to order her male guests to leave or to get them quiet. She was so terrible that early the next morning she would have a go at the three of us in the flat for being fussy and unreasonable. As far as she was concerned, she was only catching her fun, which we the boring ones didn't want.

Even though she was supposedly Muslim, she was a shame to the other Muslims in the hall, who had had enough of her, too. She did not act with any religious piety or values at all. All the hall mates finally got together and wrote to the university's head of accommodation to have her ejected, since even the security officers or wardens couldn't control her erratic behaviour.

At last, a meeting was scheduled with the head of accommodation, who wrote to her to notify her of our complaints. Of course, I bore the brunt again because she believed that I was the mastermind behind the letter. We reported all of her moves to the accommodation manager, who promised to write to her parents if her behaviour did not improve. She must have been terrified of her parents being notified, as she became a totally different person before she finally moved out after a few weeks.

Before she moved out, she gave everyone of us a piece of her mind for working against her and making her move. We had a time of jubilation when she eventually left. At least, we did live in peace.

∽

CHAPTER 16
HOORAY! FINAL CLASSES ARE HERE!

When I resumed into the Department of Biomedical Science, the courses for the final year options were: medical microbiology, cellular pathology, clinical pharmacology and clinical biochemistry, but along the way, the biochemistry option was changed to medical biochemistry rather than the clinical. On this basis, the university notified all the students formally in case anyone was bent on the clinical rather than the medical course, in which case a part refund of fees could be made.

I was impressed that they notified us of the change and offered assistance to as many as needed it as far as the course title was concerned. It reinforced the idea of students being the university's customers once again, and since we were paying for some services we deserved to get exactly what was promised.

By the final year we had few lectures on the timetable, as a high proportion of our time was designed for our personal study and research. Each student had to choose a specialist area of work. At first, I chose the medical pharmacology option, but after attending the first few lectures, which were somewhat boring, I changed my mind and opted for the medical biochemistry option. After working for a microbiology company for a year on placement, I knew straight up that microbiology wasn't the best area for me to work in.

It was unlike the second year, when we attended classes from morning till evening. It seemed great to have so much autonomy with our own study time, but the downside to it was that it took a lot of discipline to study without a programmed arrangement. It wasn't too much of a problem, since we had to meet up with our personal tutors in discussing our academic pursuits. Knowing that someone was there to check up on what I did kept me in balance.

Classes were going on fine and everyone was extremely busy with the final-year assessments, which count as seventy percent of the degree qualifications, and getting ready for the dissertation. We had more case presentations, poster making, and other coursework to hand in, as well as personal study to carry out. Funnily enough, two of my classmates were pregnant and still made it to class.

Atirah was one of the pregnant ladies. She never seemed to stop interrupting some lectures with information about the pregnancy and the stages where she was. It was either that she wanted to inform the lecturer and the whole class of the tests she had just taken or the preparations that were being made for the little one's arrival. She had a way of using her pregnant state to explain a number of things we were learning in class, which wasn't a bad idea after all, but at times I'd just feel irritated with her never-ending tales and detailed information. I felt like telling her to keep quiet and to spare us the details of what went on in her family life, but we had to put up with her.

The interesting thing about her was that she was one of those people who have a tendency to drive me nuts but laugh at the same time, so that I forget what the annoying bits are but enjoy their conversations.

Even at times when I met her in the corridors or in class and said hello, she would talk about some issues which I consider should be kept confidential. She was just a funny character who I will not forget for a long time. The baby she had in the final year was her fourth and she was still in her twenties. We just needed to ask her how her family was doing and she'd give us the low-down of the ins and outs in a few minutes, as if we were really interested in the minute details.

By the end of the first semester we had to choose our research projects, which we would undertake independently under the supervision of various lecturers. I chose to work with a female lecturer in the School of Pharmacy, carrying out some drug research by using animal models. Dr Joanne was a conscientious and friendly lecturer who offered all the help that she could with the research project.

The project involved working with rats, guinea pigs, and ferrets, so every student in her group had to undertake a Home Office animal handling course. I thought the course was mainly necessary to gain the knowledge and practical skills for handling animals, but there was much more to it. The issues of ethics and legislation concerning working with animals, coupled with the animal rights movement, made it compulsory to get adequate information and training before working with animals.

I knew of animal rights organisations and how well they protest against testing cosmetics on animals, but did not know the weight attached to scientists working with animals. During the Home Office course, we watched videos telling of scientists and research workers being attacked and in some cases killed by individuals campaigning for the rights of animals. I didn't believe how unreasonable some of these groups could be. Their main objectives seem not to be to work towards ethical and minimal use of animals in research, but a total abolition of the use of animals in research laboratories.

One such video we watched showed a group of activists who had attacked the workers on a guinea-pig-rearing farm, demanding that all such work be halted. They used sticks, clubs, and other dangerous objects in forcing their demands, while chanting went on as well. When some of them were interviewed, it was obvious that they had either been misinformed about why scientists had to be involved in animal research or they were being plain unreasonable.

A young man was asked what he felt could be used instead of animals. To display his sheer ignorance and extremism, he answered that he didn't know what alternatives were available and demanded that all animal testing be stopped.

With these violent demonstrations and behaviours, we were told not to speak about working with animals in public, lest there were animal rights activists around who might not even give us the chance to defend our actions. It seems crude that some of these activists would rather kill fellow human beings in defence of animals.

Acts like that demean human beings, lowering them from being humane to being animals themselves. I only hope that no animal rights activist reads this lest I be haunted. Can I say clearly that in the end I didn't directly work with animals myself? I was too scared and twitchy to hold them for the procedures necessary and had to change the format of my research project.

Working with Dr Joanne was indeed a pleasant experience. The materials and literature that I needed were supplied and she didn't hesitate to proofread my write-up before I submitted it for assessment. Unfortunately, she had a doctorate student named Lisa, with whom I worked in the laboratory, who had a habit of nit-picking on everything I did. It was almost like she had previously met me in another world. Even though she passed on the materials I needed from Dr Joanne to me, she played out her ugly parts mainly when Dr Joanne wasn't around, even in the presence of the other laboratory workers.

Lisa's resentment towards me became more evident after a certain incident in the university refectory. We had gone to the refectory together with some other people from the laboratory for breakfast, but before the lady behind the counter appeared, she took four pieces of sausage and some bacon into a bread roll and asked me to pick some as well. The plan was to pay for less than the number of items that we had taken, since it was a self-service section. I politely told her what my position on that was, that the action amounted to theft and my convictions and morals would not allow me to do it.

I excused myself from her side but her countenance immediately was fierce and offended. She lied about what she had picked, paid less than the actual price, and got away with it. I walked away from her but met her in the laboratory later. Maybe she thought that I was going to expose her afterwards. It's so true that people who lack integrity loathe those who uphold theirs religiously.

Lisa tried as much as she could to make life horrible for me, but I avoided her as much as I could, and I actually only had to spend a few weeks with her. By the time I was rounding up my project, she queried if all my write-up was entirely my work or if I had plagiarised anything, because she thought some of the work wasn't primarily mine and she was going to report it to the authorities.

It was a challenging experience, but I stood up to her baseless allegations because I had done my work over about eight weeks and she had no reason to assume it was plagiarised. I kept on avoiding her and went my own way thereafter.

Knowing full well that plagiarism is an offence worthy of dismissal from the university, I registered a complaint at the student's union office with the legal officer on the allegation Lisa had made, in case she made a report of it as she had threatened to do. It was obvious that all she wanted for me was to get into trouble. I informed my head of department, Dr Parks, as well. If for no other reason than to cover my back and ensure that I'd graduate at the right time with my colleagues. In this country, everything works by the law, so those who don't know their rights and the law can be treated like doormats.

Unknown to me, some of the other laboratory workers had observed Lisa's awful and hostile behaviour towards me and had informed Dr Joanne. After I handed in my dissertation, I went to Dr Joanne to thank her for her help and support throughout. She enquired about how Lisa had treated me for many weeks and why I had chosen to suffer in silence. That was how wonderful she was as a person. I explained that I didn't want to disturb her, and since I had little to do with Lisa my aim was to avoid any hoo-ha with her. She apologised for me having to put up with such behaviour and asked Lisa to apologise to me afterwards.

The next day I went into the lab to bid all the workers goodbye. Lisa walked up to me in shame and apologised for her words and terrible behaviour and told me that If I needed any help with my final examinations or other projects I could consult her for help as a friend. Who would want help from such a less-than-decent human like her? With friends like that, who needs an enemy, anyway? I appreciated her gesture, but stayed away from her whenever I saw her on campus.

By the time we finished our research projects and handed them in we had the Easter break, but there was no time to waste, so I stayed back at university to prepare for exams. The examination period was a bit stressful, with all the final touches put in and burning both ends of the candle to get the maximum results.

By the time we rounded up for the session, the only thing on everyone's mind was the graduation ball party. I looked forward to it eagerly, since I had not attended the one organised the year before. A lot of preparation was in place for the dress and the accessories to wear.

Before the final-year class dispersed, the department's lecturing professor whom we had nicknamed Father Christmas was due to retire from full-time lecturing, and it was mixed feelings that we bid him goodbye.

On the last day of his lecturing schedule, some members of staff in the department came into the class to give a farewell speech to him and gave him some gifts, too. We all joined in singing the song 'For He's A Jolly Good Fellow' and said so many of the things that he stood out for in the department. It was great ending the academic term on that jolly note.

CHAPTER 17
STUDENT POLITICS; DIRTY POLITICS

The Diaspora Association of Nigerian Students (DANS) was still active, and having been the publicity secretary the previous year, I was elected as the vice president in my final year. On resumption into the final year, it looked as though there had been a massive roll-in of Nigerian students at the university. To my surprise, the number had doubled from what we'd had in previous years. A whole block in the hall of residence was allocated mainly to the postgraduate Nigerian students and some others lived off-campus. All of a sudden, DANS had an influx of members and the society kept growing.

After a few months of our meetings, DANS decided to host other university students to an end-of-year party. That was in December of the final year. Everyone made a financial contribution to the organising of the party. We wanted other students to experience what a Nigerian party was like.

Weeks before the party, we printed leaflets and invitations and gave them out freely on campus. We got a hall, decorated it, and provided plenty of food and free-flowing drinks. We had promised not to use alcohol at all in order to send a message to fellow students about how we could have fun without necessarily taking alcohol. We knew there was a big binge-drinking problem among students.

At the same time, there was the International Students' Society (ISS), which was developing and needed executive members for her leadership. Prior to the establishment of the ISS, the only representation that international students had at the university was through the international students' student-union officer, who happened to be from another European country.

The position of the student-union officer could be filled by anyone from outside of the UK, but some of us international students felt that it was unfair for a European student to represent the international students. She couldn't fully represent our interests since she didn't pay the huge fees we paid. She wouldn't be able to identify fully with such challenges as climate adjustment, homesickness, funds transfers from another continent, and problems with communication to the home country. We felt that it would be difficult to understand our culture shocks, as well.

There were nominations for the post and all the candidates had to campaign for votes from fellow students. I was one of three nominees for the post of the president. My aim was to be a voice of the international students to the university authorities and to address some lapses I had experienced in the system.

On the day of elections, only two of the nominees for president were available, but the third candidate was mentioned in absentia. It was now time to convince the student electorate to vote me in. My opponent was a postgraduate Gambian lady who was probably in her late forties or early fifties. She'd had many years of experience working with the United Nations and other international organisations. In addition to that, she had organised and moderated various international events in her working life.

She made her passionate campaign speech to the audience before I did. She emphasised her wealth of experience and maturity as the strength she could offer the society as a leader. No doubt I had always been a leader, right from primary school, but in the presence of a highly experienced individual I momentarily felt like a dwarf. I knew that I wanted to influence certain changes in the university and that this position would be the best platform from which to do so. I therefore summoned up my courage in order to win. I believed that my God-given potential would enable me cross the hurdles before me and I needed to harness that potential in the heat of the moment.

Vested with the knowledge that most of the people in the audience were undergraduates and in the same age bracket as myself, I used that as the main weapon of my campaign. Quite all right, she had more experience than I did and she could beat me hands down on that basis, but my primary weapon could not be matched by any standard. The other weapon I had that I thought I could use was my articulate and charismatic personality.

I informed the electorate that I could identify more with them, being a young undergraduate student who had experienced what most of them were going through, and that I would articulately present their bids to the university authorities. Whao!! That did the job. I held them all spellbound throughout my campaign speech, so that I had a clapping ovation by the time I was through. Needless to say, I won! My opponent was the next runner-up, and therefore was chosen as the vice-president.

Some of my friends who heard of my campaign strategy labelled me a dirty politician. That I used a stance which a mature student could not contest in order to defeat her, but isn't that what politics is all about? It's about contesting for the votes. As long as there is no hitting below the belt in the fight, then the fight can be considered to be safe and fair.

Some other students were elected as the general secretary, publicity secretary, treasurer, IT officer, and kits officer. Together, we had a formidable combination on the team. The vice-president was indeed a great asset to the society. Her skills and experience in writing proposals and action plans were next to none. She fully supported me and helped me every step of the way.

The university's international office was firmly behind us, too. They helped in publicising meeting times and other events. By the time the society was up and running we had unanimously decided that we wanted the international students' officer to be a real international student, rather than a European or home student who had little or no idea of what we were experiencing. We expressed our views to the student-union officer, who contacted the appropriate authorities about our opinion.

The decision was that the president of the international students' society and the student-union officer would both represent the international students on the University International Students' Advisory Committee. The committee was the most powerful group in the university for making decisions about the fate of international students. That representation meant that the real views of the international students could be aired to the authorities.

We put issues on visa renewals and charges by the home office to the university authorities. We wanted the authorities to help dispatch and receive the passports back as part of the service. Even though the visa-renewal service was in place, it wasn't readily accessible to the students who needed it the most.

The other problem for which we sought an intervention by the advisory committee was the abolition of half-tuition fees for students on placement from the university. I had been fortunate because my department did not request any fee at all, but some other departments took as much as half the fees, and in some cases up to seventy percent.

The first time I raised the point, it sounded alien to most of the board members, including the international students' student-union representative, who knew next to nothing about the problem. It was important for an international student to be on the board. At first, some of the board members discouraged the motion to petition the university, saying that it was up to the various departments to charge as appropriate.

I maintained my stance as the representative of the international students who understood how difficult it could be to gather the fees, some thousands of pounds. I stated that it was unfair to be charged fees when actually the university had no responsibility or input into the students' lives while on placement. I had a few heated debates with those in the committee who insisted on the payment of fees by international students. I continually pressed them that it was unfair and unjustifiable, since the university had minimal involvement with the students while on placement.

After much deliberation, the group took the challenge on board to the university. That was a breakthrough moment for me and the society at large. That was the first feat the executive team accomplished. The next item on our agenda was to raise awareness about the representation of international students in the university student union, especially about the position of the international students' officer. What we discovered was that since a home or European student had occupied the seat of the international students' officer, most of the international students didn't know that the position was open for them to contest.

We had no problem with anyone who was in the position, but felt that it would be better suited for an international student who could identify with the day-to-day issues that we faced. For the next academic session the incumbent international students' student-union officer still occupied the position, but at least international students knew that it was open to them as well.

The weekly meetings of the ISS went on well. We took complaints and ideas down and I presented them to the advisory committee on a bi-weekly basis.

The increase in my involvement in student societies and meetings affected the amount of time I had for studying or using the library. I was usually involved in attending to one official matter or another. I knew that if I didn't balance my academic life with the societies' responsibilities well that I was headed for trouble.

I had given up my part-time job at this stage, so all I needed to focus on was my academics. I became a late-night student, always in the library till the early hours of the morning. It was such a blessing that the library stayed open twenty-four hours. All I had to sacrifice were my long sleeps. It was only a few months' sacrifice, anyway, and my body coped well.

I had many head-on collisions with the general secretary of the ISS, more than with any of the other executive members. If he wasn't late for meetings, it would be that he had stayed incommunicado for too long, or he was trying to track me down with my mobile phone during working hours. On a number of occasions we argued about various things, either the style of executing plans or time-keeping.

I tried as much as I could not to live on my mobile phones to reduce distractions to the bare minimum, especially during working hours. The general secretary didn't seem to get my drift and would try to track me down on the phone all day. Whenever he had the chance to see me on campus, the complaints were always about my attitude to the mobile phone.

We were always at loggerheads on the matter, but by the end of our term of serving on the team we had become the closest in the team and great friends. We had been through the forming, storming, norming, and performing stages of teamwork. Out of our official duties, we became very good friends and still are.

Before we dispersed for the session which was to be my final one at the university, the ISS organised a day trip to the Lake District in Cumbria. It was a splendid day out for relaxation after a harrowing examination period. We hired a coach from a local company and embarked on the two-hour trip. Riding on the boats and ferries, seeing the life of the countryside, basking in the hot sun, and having loads of treats for the day gave us the experience of British tourism.

The massive turn-out of the students was impressive. Some came with their families, and there was a feeling of ease for the journey. I had to make sure that everyone who went on the trip returned safely to the university.

On arrival in the Lake District, Windermere to be precise, everyone bought the day-tour ticket, but I received a free ticket, being the organiser and leader of the group. That was a good reward for the hard work and effort I had put into organising the trip.

By the time we were to depart in the evening, one seat on the coach was empty, meaning that one of the students was still behind. I couldn't imagine what to do at that point, since I was liable for ensuring that everyone arrived safely. As we stood there fretting over who it was and where the person was, the cheeky monkey appeared from nowhere. He had forgotten that the time for converging was long gone. Thank God! I was out of trouble. The day trip was worth the while and a good way of parting from colleagues and friends from the society.

GRADUATION BALL

The graduation ball took place a few weeks after the final exams at a hotel ballroom at the city centre. The class and the departmental representatives had organised the venue and taken our meal orders before the party. It promised to be a great experience and I wasn't disappointed afterwards.

On the evening of the ball I was picked up by two of my classmates who were as gorgeously dressed as I was. After all, this was our bespoke graduation ball and everyone wanted to appear as sparkly as possible. I wore a burgundy and black evening dress, but to my utmost surprise most of the ladies were wearing proper flowing ball gowns. It looked like a Cinderella moment with the ladies all dressed up and the guys with their bow-tie suits.

People who would not otherwise associate with one another got chatting and enjoying the night. A number of the lecturers were there and we could see them clad in their dresses and suits, too. To be honest, seeing some of the lecturers in different outfits to what I had seen them in over the years looked interesting, and in some cases hysterical. It was a pretty sight to behold.

Before we had the three-course meal we had to order our drinks at the bar individually. I didn't realise that we had to pay for the drinks at the bar, but, good as it were, different lecturers were buying drinks for the students, so there was no need to dip my hands into my purse all evening. The rapport on that day between the lecturers and students made it seem as if we were more like colleagues.

We took loads of pictures, had a great time, and later it was time to get onto the dance floor, so many people got on, while a handful, including me, watched the various dance steps being exhibited from the back. It was funny to see the lecturers all on the dance floor.

That evening a female professor in the department especially became the centre of attention. She was a real stepper and displaced even the younger ones. At one stage she was being watched and hailed as she got busy with her dance steps. A group of us were laughing as hard as we could. It was unbelievable how well she could dance and how she beat the students to it. One could only imagine what she had been like in her younger days.

As the night went by, the drunken ones started to appear on the scene. It's almost as if any social event involving students isn't accomplished until the drinking sessions are introduced. Under the influence of booze, various dances were invented and displayed. Some of them were funny, but some others were weird and strange. I left as soon as the whole programme was through, but had caught enough of the fun to add it to my memoirs. It was an evening worthy of remembering.

∽

CHAPTER 18
PART-TIME JOBS

By the time I settled into the university hall, I needed to pay back the loan I took out from the students' finance and information services, so I needed to get a job fast. I tried getting a job from the university job shop, where students get to apply for as many jobs as possible. The jobs could be on-campus or in industries in the city. Bradford, being a highly industrialised city, has many industries where a number of students took up part-time manual jobs. I had been advised by some colleagues not to get a job in a manufacturing industry because it could be too tiring. I took their advice and sought other jobs.

After a few weeks of searching, I finally got a job at the city college cleaning and tidying up the library. It was an early-morning job between 7.30 am and 9.30 am on weekdays. It was a relatively easy job, but I missed my first hour of lectures every day. I quit this job after a few weeks to concentrate on my academics. I didn't even tell my parents that I had taken up such a costly job. At that stage I was introduced to recruitment agencies in the city.

I didn't understand how recruitment agencies worked at the time, but I was keen on getting a job, so I went to some of the offices and asked them for jobs upfront. They informed me that I had to fill out their application forms and they would notify me if they had shifts or posts in the future. I was disappointed, since I believed that the agencies could get me to work straight away. I registered with about four agencies and waited for them to get me some shifts with their various clients.

Sure, the agencies gave me shifts, but they were highly erratic, unpredictable, and impromptu most of the time. They would ring for me to work somewhere on the day, but with a notice as short as one hour. I realised that working for agencies as a temporary worker was as good as waiting on the climate for weather changes. It was impossible to know exactly what to expect. I continually worked for them as a kitchen assistant whenever I was called upon, but I knew that I needed a steady job.

Recruitment agencies, being profit-making organisations, place job-seeking employees into employment and charge the employers or companies for doing so. Most employment agencies are located on the high streets and they pay on an hourly basis. More often than not, employment agencies deal with specific sectors, such as the food, medical, nursing, or construction industries.

The main aim of employment agencies is to make profits by working with job seekers and employers, and therefore they have multiple candidates at any given time. If one is able to develop a rapport and relationship with them over the phone, they are more likely to give that individual more shifts and better working environments.

It's only human nature for the employment consultant to contact the person who is closer to him or her over the phone for a post than a random person on the database. With that in mind, I tried to keep in close communication with those people on a regular basis. I knew their first names and would always request to speak to the ones with whom I had developed personal relationships whenever I called their offices for shifts.

In the hospital kitchen where I worked, most of us from that agency were university students, and we were often expected to do a lot more than the permanent workers. More often than not, permanent workers seem to believe that agency staff are better paid than they are and should thus be assigned the toughest tasks.

It was all going on well until one of the supervisors asked me to stay behind to carry out some duties after my contracted working hours. Being an evening time job, I needed to catch the bus at a designated time and explained the situation to her. I could tell that she wasn't happy that I had to leave. I had no choice than to catch the bus, which commuted that route only on an hourly basis at that time of the evening. I didn't feel that anything was amiss, considering that the duties she allocated to me were out of my normal working hours, anyway.

Unknown to me, she had requested from the agency that I should not be sent back to work in the hospital. Actually, she had lied about the reason for her request to the agency staff member, who was kind enough to explain the situation to me. On telling my side of the story, Rita, the recruitment assistant, told me not to worry, but got me some better shifts elsewhere. Truly, God was with me every step of the way. The need for a permanent part-time job was pressing at this stage.

If only some people back home understood the difficulties and hardship one encounters in the workplace abroad, maybe the incessant demands for money and other material goods would be rightly put into perspective. If it wasn't a difficult supervisor like that, it could be another work colleague, who would work tirelessly to get me dismissed. Life isn't gimmicks, but it could be tougher for those are foreigners in a country.

I had always loved to work directly with people, and a job caring for the elderly appealed greatly to me. Close to the university, there was a care home for the elderly which I saw while passing by on a regular basis.

One day I walked into the nursing home and asked to see the proprietor or manager. A middle-aged blonde lady named Alice attended to me and introduced herself to me as the proprietress. She and her husband, James, jointly ran and managed the nursing home. On mentioning my name, she knew straight away that I was Nigerian and took a special interest in me. I introduced myself to her and expressed my interest in working in their care home, subject to the availability of vacancies. Unfortunately, there was no vacancy, but she took down my details to contact me if any ever came up.

Alice and James had lived in Nigeria for many years before settling back in the UK. According to her, they'd had an excellent time living among Nigerians, and she specially liked the local dishes, which she asked me about. The excitement with which she spoke to me about her Nigerian experience proved that they'd really had a wonderful time there. I felt particularly proud of being a Nigerian at that moment, and we chatted on that first day as if we already knew each other. It seemed she had taken up much of the friendly, accommodating, and exuberant Nigerian attitude while she'd lived out there.

A week after my meeting with Alice, she telephoned me and offered me a job straightaway. There was no formal interview scheduled, and she was willing to give me the training that I needed. All I had to do was to give her my lecture timetable so she could know when I could work in the home. She was a lovely and wonderful lady and her husband had a similar personality. They were marvellousy understanding and offered me all the assistance that they could as far as working with them was concerned. If they'd had a terrible experience in Nigeria, though, I can imagine how they might have treated me.

I was enjoying the job and the people I worked with until things started becoming rough with Debbie, the matron-in-charge. After I was introduced to her, she enquired about my nationality and my status in the country. On telling her that I was Nigerian I noticed that her countenance changed immediately. I couldn't figure out what was going on, and so left things that way.

The next time I worked with her she questioned me further on where I was from in Nigeria, and if I knew certain cities in the country. She told me of her experience of living in Nigeria almost thirty years before I met her. According to her, she had just graduated from the school of nursing when she met a young Nigerian doctor with whom she fell in love. One thing led to another and they got married in the UK. At the time, she was around twenty-one years of age, naïve and innocent.

A few months after their marriage the Nigerian husband wanted to relocate to Nigeria and she went along with him in the hope that she was building her life and home with the man she loved.

Unknown to her, the man had three other wives in Nigeria, who were introduced to her at the outset as his sisters. What she couldn't understand was why the three sisters had to live in the same house with them as a newlywed couple.

After a few months of questioning the man, he revealed the secret to her. That the women were actually his first three wives and that she, Debbie, was actually an addition to his harem as the fourth.

On knowing the dilemma she was in, Debbie tried to escape from this devious man, but he knew of her plans and confiscated her passport. The time she spent in his house back in Nigeria was a tormenting period of being grounded in a foreign country. According to her, she eventually contacted the British High Commission in Nigeria, who came to her rescue before she escaped back to her family into the UK.

After that harrowing experience, she never ventured into marriage again, but kept to herself as a result of the betrayal and horror she once experienced. As she told me her story, which was almost thirty years old, I could sense a deep sense of bitterness and anger in her voice towards the man, and maybe Nigerians in general. Before I knew it, she started to pick on me for no real reasons.

If it wasn't that I wasn't fast enough in dealing with the residents, it was usually the complaint of not cleaning well enough. I could somehow explain why she acted in such a manner towards me, but I didn't feel that her horrific experience with a Nigerian man could excuse her hostile attitude towards me.

That mixed experience just showed me how people could act towards me based on their experiences with those that they had encountered previously who have similarities to me. The bliss that James and Alice enjoyed in Nigeria turned out well for me, but Debbie's awful encounter made her sour towards me. I considered all of that to be part of living in a realist's world rather than as an idealist.

After a few weeks she had made some reports about me to James saying that she didn't want to work with me any further. James made all these known to me and advised me to look for another job. He said that he knew that I did a good job, but since the matron in charge had some issues with me it was better for me to leave voluntarily rather than being incriminated at a later stage. He apologised for the occurrence but promised to give me a good reference whenever I needed one.

I thanked James for his kind gesture and advice, but felt that it was unfair for me to have to leave the job, especially when there was nothing concrete that I had done wrong. The only problem was that Debbie didn't want to work with me. Maybe I was a reminder of the terrible experience that she'd had in Nigeria. Throughout the time that I worked in that care home I didn't work for any of the recruitment agencies, but I decided to contact them again to see if they could get me shifts. Moreover, James and Alice gave me no notice of the termination of my employment.

The disappointment I felt from a couple who were once kind to me was indescribable, but I decided to move on from there and to hold nothing against them. After all, they had offered their help when

I needed it most, and working in a hostile environment with Debbie wasn't the best situation, after all.

I left the care home and went to a friend in the hall of residence to discuss the situation with someone who could empathise with me. I had not even contacted any recruitment agency yet when I received a telephone call in my friend's house from a recruitment agent I had registered with a few months earlier. He wanted to know if I was interested in a three-month contract which he had available in a nursing home in Leeds.

I immediately registered my interest, since it was only two night shifts a week and the pay was double what I had earned when I worked for James and Alice. The night shifts meant that I could spend more time on campus and in the library, and I was more organised with the part-time job. I became ecstatic and was over the moon for the offer. Indeed, the heavens were smiling on me and I didn't need any comfort again from my friend in whose room I was. That was an immediate answer to my prayers. God must have seen the unfairness and decided to reward me with a better deal.

The contract in Leeds was fantastic and comfortable. I worked with a bunch of nice people and came back to Bradford in the mornings after the shifts. In no time, the three-month period was over and I was preparing for the second semester examinations. I decided not to work as I prepared for the exams. As soon as the examination was over I went off to London for the summer holidays.

Summer was a great time to save up for the next session, but getting another job was a hassle. Eventually, I got a summer job in a nursing home not too far from where my family lived. The manager of the house was a really pleasant lady who took an interest in my academic life. She was impressed with my background and my course of study.

She asked me what options were available to me on completion of my degree and I informed her that it could be a route into medical school, where I could qualify as a medical doctor. Immediately I told her about that, she said she believed that I would do well as a medical doctor and encouraged me to pursue that path if I could.

I was shown round the home and she introduced me to all the members of staff and residents as a doctor to be. Inasmuch as I tried to tell her that it was only an option to be considered, she seemed keen on introducing me as such. In no time, most of the people in the home started to refer to me as a doctor-in-the-making. No explanation I gave sufficed, as it seemed like they had already made up their minds about me.

What impressed me most about the manager's attitude was her enthusiasm in knowing that I was ambitious and focused in life. Contrary to the common attitude I had observed among the British people, who have this Pull-him-or-her-Down (PhD) attitude towards achievers and ambitious people, the manager was excited about a young lady with dreams and aspirations in life. I have come to call the UK a PhD society, where successful and aspiring people are often bad-mouthed and scorned. This PhD syndrome isn't just targeted towards foreigners, but to the natives as well. Of course, that effect is only multiplied when it comes to dealing with foreigners.

The governmental system and the private sector seek to reward achievers in various fields, but in everyday life the general populace seems to design ways to frustrate achievers. If a person does well in any sphere of life, that person can be sure to gain more enemies than friends compared to anyone who chooses to be stagnant and unfocused. Being ordinary and common is the accepted norm, so when someone seeks to break out of that mould they receive heavy criticisms, cynical comments, and sarcasm from the general public. It seems to be such a shame.

I worked well in that nursing home and the manager never stopped encouraging and challenging me throughout the summer. She always told me to be the best in whatever my is endeavour in life and to make the most of my youth. At times I almost found it difficult to believe that she was British. She showed me the accepting and encouraging side to British life. People like her make us see the other side of the coin that we might not have seen before.

Most of the people I had worked with prior to that had usually been up-tight when they discovered that I was working on something tangible with my life. It was almost as if I had stolen something from them for desiring to be somebody. I guess individuals who have stopped developing themselves in different facets of life see ambitious and visionary people as threats, and they express that in cold-shoulder attitudes and resentment. That manager was a phenomenal and exceptional woman.

When the summer was over I moved back to Bradford to take up my post in the industrial laboratory for my one-year placement. When the placement period came to an end I returned for my final year at university, but I had to give up my part-time jobs as a result of my many commitments at the time.

My experience of working part-time was absolutely invaluable because I came to understand the British workplace culture and the attitudes of the people to different issues. Even though the maximum number of hours that an international student could work during term-times was twenty, I felt that it was okay as long as I avoided any conflict of interests with my main purpose of studying.

Working part-time also availed me the opportunity to be responsible for myself and to learn how to live on a tight budget. If my entire stipend had come only from my parents I doubt if I would have learnt the many survival tactics that I gained within my three years at university. It was a great experience that stretched me and made me more mature than I was on enrolment into the university.

∽

CHAPTER 19
MORE CULTURE SHOCKS

Some of the culture shocks I experienced during my first few months in the UK were totally unimaginable or comprehensible for me. From the communicative patterns to food culture and family life, I was faced with so many culture shocks which opened me up into the new system.

If the hokey-kokey friendly approaches weren't familiar, I was faced with the non-confrontational nature of the British people. It took me a while to understand how unconfrontational people would be about issues affecting them, but how they would gladly discuss these issues out of the sight of the perpetrator. If, for example, someone jumped ahead in a queue or acted out of order in a public place, I'd observe that hardly anyone would complain there and then. I would only observe the subsequent reactions of moaning and whispered chit-chats about it.

Even if someone was being beaten to death in a public place by some unruly yobs, we'd observe members of the public staying out of it and pretending that nothing significant was occurring. That type of behaviour is totally different to what I had experienced back home. People don't even need to notify the public authorities to intervene in instances of unruly behaviour; if a person is accosted as a thief or thug in a public place the general public could go as far as lynching that person.

Of course, members of the public taking the law into their own hands is erratic and totally unacceptable in a law-abiding society, but the extremes of both societies show how different people are groomed to act in public. Whilst Nigerians could be more prone to act to defend the victim, the British would act in utmost denial.

An encounter that buttressed my opinion of this non-confrontational nature of the British people was an incident that occurred at the train station in Bradford. It was during my first few weeks at university when I commuted from Leeds to Bradford daily. On that fateful evening I was on the train platform with other commuters waiting for the arrival of the train to Leeds. An elderly man who was a newspaper vendor came onto the platform to advertise the dailies, to which I showed a lack of interest.

A few feet away from me was a young girl who beckoned to the vendor so she could look through the newspaper pages. Her attitude suggested that she was interested in buying the newspaper, which the man agreed to. After a number of minutes, she returned the newspaper to the vendor and told him to excuse her. That was after perusing the newspaper from front to back and acting as though she was interested. Naturally, the vendor got upset and gave her a piece of his mind as he walked away.

That teenage girl wasn't going to lay the issue to rest. She began to rant and insult the elderly vendor with every insolent word under the heavens. To my greatest shock, nobody older around or on the train platform called her to order or tried stopping her as she threw her tantrum. Gosh! My mouth was wide agape in shock. The worst part of it was that the girl did not see anything wrong in her disgraceful behaviour in public.

A few minutes after that baffling episode, the train arrived and we all boarded to Leeds. I intentionally moved into the same carriage with the girl in order to have a word with her about her erratic and rude behaviour. I approached her in a down-to-earth manner and enquired from her why she had spoken in such a rude manner to the elderly man, knowing full well that he was much older than she was. She tried brushing my point off, but I was more than ready to engage her in this serious conversation.

When she realised that I wasn't going to leave her alone, she got a bit more relaxed, introduced herself to me as Matilda, and demanded to know why I was so interested in her. I introduced myself to her and we got into the conversation. In the same friendly manner, I gave her a thorough tutorial as to why her behaviour was unacceptable and too rude for keeps. By the time we got to Leeds, we had engaged in a meaningful conversation and she said she felt apologetic for her attitude towards the elderly vendor.

Good as it was, we headed for the same bustop in Leeds and needed to catch the same bus home. Our instantaneous friendship was moving onto another level in only a few minutes. I am sure she was convinced that I wasn't willing to let go of her that evening. As a student fresh from Africa just then, to me Matilda's behaviour that evening seemed to be an abomination

Matilda was a fifteen-year-old secondary-school dropout who lived with her grandparents because she had become too difficult for her parents to handle. She told me of her decision to quit schooling because she believed that it wasn't for someone like her and that she didn't have the brains for academics. Guess what she thought she was suited for? Your guess might be as good as mine: modelling or a musical career.

Remember, by the time I met Matilda I had barely spent two months in the UK and the idea of a teenager believing that formal education wasn't suited for her was strange to me. Little did I know that many teenagers in this country think in the same way. All they are interested in seems to be becoming the next football icon, supermodel, or pop singer. I was terribly shocked that she was not staying out of school because of financial restraints or lack of resources, but due to sheer lassitude.

I asked her many more questions about herself and where she was coming from at that time of the night. It was around ten o'clock in the evening, and I asked if her grandparents weren't going to be bothered by her lateness. Her response was that she had her life to live and nobody could interfere with what she wanted. She had actually travelled to Bradford to see her boyfriend, who was in his twenties. If it was in my country, a girl would have to give tenable reasons to her guardian for staying out of school at that age, and her business being out late in the evening visiting a boyfriend.

As Matilda and I discussed things further, I asked her what she did with her time during the day, since she didn't go to school and was too young to hold down a job. According to her, she spent her days chilling and hanging out with friends. She continued by saying that they went out for drinks and had good times. I found it difficult to believe that a fifteen-year-old girl drank alcohol and smoked.

When I actually asked her if she smoked, she said that she didn't smoke tobacco because she believed that it adversely affects the brain, and that the only thing she smoked was marijuana. At that point I couldn't hide my response that her revelations were damn shocking to me. Even the way she pronounced marijuana, which I didn't get clearly, made it sound like she said mariwana. When I asked her to repeat what she meant, she answered, "I smoke weed but not cigs, because cigs are bad for the brain."

My goodness! It felt like I was momentarily going to jump out of my skin as Matilda narrated the other vices that constituted the cool and trendy social life for which she had swapped her education. I felt like she needed some proper disciplining, which might be considered to be abusive in a country like this. If at fifteen years of age she had experimented with men, drugs, booze, and truancy, I wondered what she would be up to by the time she reached twenty-one, unless a miraculous turn-around came into her life.

Was I in for more shocks? Every now and then I'd walk down the road and see these tiny little ones kissing passionately in public. I found it strange that people found it easy to snog, kiss, and fondle in public. Plain disgusting! Why they don't get appropriate venues for their displays of so-called love, or better still, lust, was totally beyond me. Fortunately, I wasn't the only one who found this common attitude disgusting. A number of international students I hung out with also found it bizarre. At one stage I thought the government should promulgate a law to prohibit indecent and illicit displays of affection in public.

The worst bit of this snogging culture is that I saw children as young as twelve at the bus stops passionately kissing and fondling each other. It beggars questioning how they were brought up and how they display no shame whatsoever as they get down to these disgusting acts. This is everyday life in the UK. Children seem to get away with most wrong behaviour and get involved in such vices as smoking and binge-drinking, even in the presence of adults. Any adult who dares to say a word could be labelled as being abusive .

Back in Nigeria, a sense of reverence toward adults inhibits certain behavioural traits in children. Even if a child is tempted to act waywardly, the presence of an adult who could discipline him or her is a deterrent. That doesn't seem to happen over here.

Another major culture shock which I faced in my early days in the UK was people smiling at me even when they disdained me and thought ill of me. There seems to be this trait in Britain that people don't display their true emotions, which means that even when they're mad at a person, they still put up this fake smile so as to come across as being nice. Even when a person is set to antagonise others, that person would still smile with them until they are placed in the coffin carved out for them.

Before I understood this British trait I used to think that the smiles meant that I was welcomed and accepted, but as I looked a bit deeper I realised that many of those smiles could be better described as grins, or fake smiles. It was difficult to understand that a person that clearly works against my stance would still smile and pretend to be on my side up to the moment that I discovered the tactics.

In some cases this attitude is said to be diplomatic, but for someone like me who grew up in a Nigerian society where people speak their minds plainly it was tough to comprehend the rationale behind the grins and fake smiles. Among Africans generally, and most especially in Nigeria, we don't need an angel to announce our friends to us, and neither do we need a prophet to forewarn us of an enemy. We just know what we're up against. If people don't like us, they don't go to the extent of smiling and offering us a cup of tea. They show us clearly that we're not accepted and it's be up to us to take it or leave it. After living in the UK for a few years, I think I can now differentiate between the phoney and genuine smiles to an extent. This phenomenon is simple, but it seems it is something a number of foreigners in the UK, such as myself, find particularly difficult to comprehend.

The African person's inclination would be to ask, "Why waste my time making an effort to smile when I know that I don't like this individual?" On the other hand, the Briton's inclination would be to think, "It's only civil to put up a smile, albeit fake, rather than express exactly how I feel upfront." Expressing the way people feel outright isn't something we'd be likely to observe among Brits. Different cultures have different interpretations to issues and different approaches

One other cultural issue I questioned in my early days in the UK is the way people generally address each other. Besides the lecturers, whom we addressed by their titles, most people call each other by their first names. Even in official settings, most people would introduce themselves to me by their first names rather than by Mr, Mrs, or Dr. Junior members of staff would address their seniors by their first names irrespective of the age differences. Contrary to our African cultures, where we generally refer to people by their titles and surnames, the UK has adopted an informal and laid-back approach. Addressing people in this manner didn't feel right at first, especially if they were older than I was. Even children call their friends' parents by their first names, which I considered to be absurd. The African way of referring to anyone older than oneself as Aunty or Uncle was what I was used to and expecting.

This other culture shock is one that most foreign students face in the course of living in the UK. I was brought up in a culture where older people in the community are highly respected and so revered that we don't look them straight in the eyes when they are speaking to us. To the contrary, if someone is speaking to someone else in the British culture it is impolite to look away from them, irrespective of their age. The proof of paying attention to the person would be in looking him or her straight in the eyes and maintaining close eye contact throughout the conversation

It was challenging for someone from my kind of background to adjust to looking at a senior person straight in the eyes. The ideal manner of communication would then be to look sideways or down a bit, rather than with the face staring up. One of my African work colleagues almost got into trouble with a manager who complained that she rudely looked away from her when being spoken to. What the manager did not realise was that the lady was only being polite in her own way.

The longer I lived in the UK, the more shocking attitudes I acquired, and with time I became adjusted to the once strange and absurd ways of British life. After a number of years, I haven't fully identified with some of those cultural traits, but I think I can relate to them better and with clearer understanding now.

These are the tales of an international student in the UK. Some of the experiences are hilarious, some challenging, and others intriguing, irritating, and exciting. Welcome aboard to the UK.

AUTHOR BIOGRAPHY

The author, Olanike Adebayo was born in Abeokuta, Nigeria in West Africa where she grew up before she relocated to the UK. She bagged a degree in Biomedical Science from the University of Bradford in 2005.

While studying at the university, she served as the president of the International Students' Society as well as the vice –president of the Diaspora association of Nigerian students.

Olanike is a member of the Freelance writers, UK and She works in London as a scientist.

3743456

Made in the USA